THE WRETCHED "I" AND ITS LIBERATION

PAUL IN ROMANS 7 AND 8

Louvain Theological and Pastoral Monographs is a publishing venture whose purpose is to provide those involved in pastoral ministry throughout the world with studies inspired by Louvain's long tradition of theological excellence within the Roman Catholic Tradition. The volumes selected for publication in the series are expected to express some of today's finest reflection on current theology and pastoral practice.

Members of the Editorial Board

The Executive Committee:

Raymond F. Collins, Catholic University of Leuven, chairman
Thomas P. Ivory, The American College, Catholic University of Leuven
Joël Delobel, Catholic University of Leuven
Lambert Leijssen, Catholic University of Leuven
Terrence Merrigan, Catholic University of Leuven, secretary

Members at Large:

Raymond E. Brown, Union Theological Seminary, New York
Juliana Casey, The Catholic Health Association of the United States
José M. de Mesa, East Asian Pastoral Institute, Manila, Philippines
Catherine Dooley, The Catholic University of America
Mary Grey, The Catholic University of Nijmegen, the Netherlands
James J. Kelly, Trinity College, Dublin, Ireland
Maria Goretti Lau, Holy Spirit Study Centre, Hong Kong
Donatus Mathenge, Nyeri Catholic Secretariat, Nyeri, Kenya
Michael Putney, Pius XII Provincial Seminary, Banyo, Australia
Ronald Rolheiser, Newman Theological College, Edmonton, Alberta, Canada
Donald P. Senior, Catholic Theological Union, Chicago
James J. Walter, Loyola University of Chicago

LOUVAIN THEOLOGICAL & PASTORAL MONOGRAPHS
14

THE WRETCHED "I" AND ITS LIBERATION

PAUL IN ROMANS 7 AND 8

Jan Lambrecht, S.J.

PEETERS PRESS
LOUVAIN

W.B. EERDMANS

Translated and adapted from *Het verscheurde 'ik' en zijn bevrijding. Paulus in Romeinen 7 en 8*, Leuven: VBS/Acco, 1992.

The vignette on the cover is a reproduction of a Saint Paul mosaic from Rome.

ISBN 90-6831-436-X
D. 1992/0602/72

TABLE OF CONTENTS

FOREWORD 9

CHAPTER ONE
Sin and Law (Romans 3:1-8; 6:1-14 and 6:15-7:6) . . . 13-27

I. Continuation in Sin? 13
    Let Us Do Evil (Romans 3:1-8) 13
    Shall We Persist in Sin? (Romans 6:1-14) 16
    Are We to Sin? (Romans 6:15-7:6) 18

II. The Law Which Came Later 22
    The Law Brings Knowledge of Sin 23
    Transgression of the Law Calls for Punishment . . . 23
    The Law Arouses Sinful Desires 24

III. Sin and the Law in Current Exegesis 24
    Sin 25
    The Law 25

CHAPTER TWO
Romans 7:7-25: Its Structure and Line of Thought . . . 29-42

I. The Structure 31
    The Diatribe Style 31
    The Inclusion (Romans 7:6 and 8:2) 33
    An Interruption in the Text (Romans 7:12 and 13) . 34
    The End of the Pericope (Romans 7:24-8:1) 35

II. The Line of Thought 37
    The First Part (Romans 7:7-12) 37
    The Second Part (Romans 7:13-25) 38

III. Remarks and Questions 40
    Text and Context 40
    The "I" 41

CHAPTER THREE
Romans 7:7-25: Exegesis 43-57

I. The First Part (Romans 7:7-12) 43
    Sin and the Law (vv. 7-8) 43
    The Tragic Event (vv. 9-11) 46
    The Conclusion (v. 12) 48

II. The Second Part (Romans 7:13-25) 48
    The Fleshly "I" (vv. 13-14) 49
    The Conflict Within the "I" (vv. 15-20) 52
    The Diagnosis (vv. 21-23) 53
    "Simul iustus et pecccator?" (vv. 24-25) 54

III. Epilogue and Questions 55

CHAPTER FOUR
Who is That "I"? Several Proposals 59-72

I. Four Basic Proposals 59
    Paul Himself 59
    Adam 62
    Israel or the Jews Under the Law 64
    Christians 65

II. Composite Proposals 67
    Fusion 67
    The Psychological "I" 68

III. Brief Conclusion 72

CHAPTER FIVE
The Identity of the "I" 72-91

I. Does Paul Mean Himself? 74
    A Rhetorical "I" 74
    To a Great Extent Autobiographical 75
    Transgression of the Law 79

II. Allusions to Salvation History 80
    Paul's Own Growth? 80
    The Fall of Adam 82
    Unredeemed Israel 84

III. Existential Character	85
A Retrospective of the Unregenerate Past	86
Relevance for the Christian Future	87
IV. Conclusion	89

CHAPTER SIX
Christian Certainty of Salvation (Romans 8:1-17 and 31-39)   93-113

I. Led by the Spirit (Romans 8:1-17)	94
The Text	95
The Line of Thought	98
The Indwelling Spirit	100
II. Nothing Can Separate Us from the Love of God (Romans 8:31-39)	102
A First Reading of the text	103
Content	107
Certainty?	108
If God Is for Us ...	111

CHAPTER SEVEN
Creation Which Groans (Romans 8:19-22)   115-133

I. Train of Thought	116
The Textual Unit	117
Content	118
II. Explanation	120
Verses 18-22	120
Verses 23-25	122
Verses 26-27	123
Verses 28-30	124
III. The Future of the World	126
Does Creation Groan?	127
Rupture or Union?	130
The Commission	132

CHAPTER EIGHT
Critical and Actualizing Observations 135-139

    Two Considerations 136
    Relevance for Christians Today 138

APPENDIX
Four Modern Translations 141-158

BIBLIOGRAPHY 159-165

FOREWORD

In his recent commentary on Paul's letter to the Romans (1989), John A. Ziesler wrote that the "I" of the seventh chapter has received "so much scholarly attention ... with so little resulting agreement" (p. 179). One could be amazed at such a remark. After all, in his monograph of 1929 *Römer 7 und die Bekehrung des Paulus*, Werner G. Kümmel was considered by many to have proven forever that by "I" Paul did not mean himself, nor the Christian, but men and women before and without Christ. Looking at numerous recent publications, however, one soon realizes that the discussion goes on. Whom and what does Paul mean when he says: I do not what I want but the very thing I hate, or: I know that nothing good dwells within me (see Romans 7:15 and 18)? How must we understand what is said in 8:2: "For the law of the Spirit of life in Christ Jesus has set you free from the law of sin and of death"?

In Roman Catholic liturgy the situation of Romans 7 is quite strange. While in the three Sunday cycles (A, B and C) ten passages from Romans 8 are used, not a single text from Romans 7 occurs as a liturgical reading on Sundays (or feastdays). For weekdays five pericopes are taken from Romans 8, but only one from Romans 7. This situation alone provides a sufficient reason to make this famous seventh chapter better known through written comment.

In 1974 we devoted a publication to Romans 7:7-25: "Man Before and Without Christ: Rom 7 and Pauline Anthropology" in *Louvain Studies* 5 (1974-75) 18-33. In the present book we expand that study and add an investigation of its context, as well as a detailed treatment of

Romans 8. In Romans 7 and 8 Paul deals with the wretched "I" and its liberation.

In 7:7, the verse which introduces the pericope with "I," Paul asks whether the law is sin. In the first chapter, therefore, we consider the passages before Romans 7 which point to a connection between law and sin. In the second and third chapters we analyze Romans 7:7-25: first the structure and line of thought, then the exegetical difficulties which are present in this passage. In chapters four and five the question of the "I" is under discussion. In the fourth chapter we provide an overview of the principal explanations and in the fifth we present and defend our own view. The sixth chapter deals with the passages from Romans 8 in which Paul speaks of the liberation of those who are in Christ, and of the life that they must live. The seventh chapter is taken from *Louvain Studies* 15 (1990) 3-18 (without the footnotes); in a slightly revised form it examines Romans 8:18-30, more particularly verses 19-22. The reader will notice its outspoken "ecological" focus. In chapter eight we critically reflect upon what Paul has worked out in Romans 7 and 8; we will also try to point out the relevancy of these texts for Christians today.

The Bible translation used in this book is that of the New Revised Standard Version, except for some passages where the close examination requires a more literal version. In an appendix we bring together four modern translations, verse after verse, for the sake of comparison. In addition to commentaries on Romans (for the most part recent), the bibliography at the end of the book includes only monographs and articles which directly treat Romans 7 and 8. Within the text the references use the name of the author (and, if necessary, also an abbreviated title). This book was first published in Dutch: *Het verscheurde 'ik' en zijn bevrij-*

ding. Paulus in Romeinen 7 en 8 (Leuven: VBS/Acco, 1992). At the completion of this translation I wish to sincerely thank Dr. Veronica Koperski, SFCC, for correcting the English. I also wish to express my gratitude to the members of the Executive Committee and especially the chairman, Professor Raymond E. Collins, who accepted the book in the *Louvain Theological and Pastoral Monographs* series.

While writing this monograph a double question was alive within me. What did Paul mean in this section of his letter and what is the significance of these Pauline passages for modern Christians? I hope that the effort needed to answer the first question does not make us lose sight of the answer to the second. Since the coming of Jesus the wretched "I" has been set free. Nothing and nobody can separate the Christian from the love of God which is in Christ Jesus our Lord. However each Christian has the terrifying possibility of doing that. Paul has written Romans 7 and 8 so as, by God's grace, to remove this danger from his brother and sister Christians.

Leuven, 29 June 1992,
on the Feast of Peter and Paul, Apostles.   J.L.

CHAPTER ONE

Sin and Law
(Romans 3:1-8; 6:1-14 and 6:15-7:6)

What Paul writes about the division within the "I" in Romans 7:7-25 is difficult to understand. For a correct interpretation we need the help of the context of the letter. How has Paul arrived at the vexing question of 7:7 whether sin and law are one and the some thing? A double consideration may be helpful, first about sin, then about the law.

I. Continuation in Sin?

Before Romans 7:7-25 Paul had already spoken in three passages of sinning or doing evil after justification. In 3:8 he cites what some people slanderously report him as saying: "Let us do evil so that good may come." In 6:1 he asks the question: "Should we continue in sin in order that grace may abound?" In 6:15, finally, he again asks: "Should we sin because we are not under law but under grace?"

Let Us Do Evil! (Romans 3:1-8)

From the whole of Romans 2:18-3:20 it appears that sin eradicates the difference between Jew and Gentile. Jews who sin are not better than Gentiles. And, the other way round, Gentiles who observe the requirements of the law are as good as the Jews. "A person is a Jew who is one inwardly, and real circumcision is a matter of the heart ..." (2:29). The readers react:

> *3:1 "Then what advantage has the Jew? Or what is the value of circumcision?"*
> *2 Much, in every way. For in the first place the Jews were entrusted with the oracle of God.*
> *3 "What if some were unfaithful? Will their faithlessness nullify the faithfulness of God?"*
> *4 By no means! Although everyone is a liar, let God be proved true, as it is written, 'So that you may be justified in your words, and prevail in your judging' (Ps 51:6).*
> *5 "But if our injustice serves to confirm the justice of God, what should we say? That God is unjust to inflict wrath on us?" (I speak in a human way.)*
> *6 By no means! For then how could God judge the world?*
> *7 But if through my falsehood God's truthfulness abounds to his glory, why am I still being condemned as a sinner?*
> *8 And why not say (as some people slander us by saying that we say), "Let us do evil so that good may come"? Their condemnation is deserved!*

From 2:25-29 we know that being circumcised and possessing the law are subordinated to observing the law. If there is no observance, circumcision is tantamount to uncircumcision; being circumcised no longer has any value. Over and against this it is stated that keeping the law without circumcision is regarded as being circumcised. 3:1 continues the discussion: Then what advantage have the Jews, that is: in view of all this what is the value of circumcision? Paul answers positively and emphatically. He begins an enumeration which, however, is immediately broken off by new, lively questions. By "God's oracles" in verse 2 Paul in the first place means the covenantal promises of God. Paul is thinking of Israel's undeserved election, of her salvation historical privileges.

In verses 3-8 there are three (double) questions. They result from a reasoning through to its logical conclusion. They intend to show that Paul's position is indefensible and his system untenable.
(1) First God's faithfulness is dealt with (vv. 3-4). God may entrust the Jews with oracles, but is God's faithfulness not canceled by the faithlessness of some Jews? Paul's answer is: "Certainly not, by no means!"
(2) Then the text speaks of God's punishment (vv. 5-6). Thus, the opponents continue, our injustice serves to evoke God's salvific justice. Is God then not unjust to inflict wrath on sinners? The emotional answer is again: "Certainly not, by no means!"
(3) Finally the opponents focus on moral life (vv. 7-8). They insist: If my falsehood procures all the greater glory for God's truth, why should I any longer be condemned as a sinner and why not do evil in order that good may come? Paul notes that this third objection contains words and ideas which are falsely ascribed to him. Such people, Paul says, are condemned because of their slander, and they deserve it.

The weakness of Paul's answer is evident; it cannot but strike the readers of this text. The opponents are reduced to silence, first by means of an exclamation, then through a dogmatic appeal to what the Jew should believe from Scripture (God's faithfulness and God's competence as judge) and, finally, by stressing that the accusation is false.

Moreover, in the same chapter, after the solemn statement that a person is justified by faith, not by keeping the law (see v. 28), the question is asked: "Do we then overthrow the law by this faith" (v. 31a). Paul's answer is perfectly clear: "On the contrary, we uphold the law" (v. 31b). Yet, the readers remain puzzled and perplexed. How must they understand this answer in the light of what has been said about the law a moment ago?

Shall We Persist in Sin? (Romans 6:1-14)

In the letter to the Romans we come across the same conclusion with regard to sinning after justification. In 5:20 Paul writes that grace became immeasurably great there where sin increased. In 6:1 the conclusion from the assertion is drawn in question form: Shall we persist in sin, so that there may be all the more grace? We must read the whole of Romans 6:1-14:

> *6:1 What then are we to say? Should we continue in sin in order that grace may abound?*
> *2 By no means! How can we who died to sin go on living in it?*
> *3 Do you not know that all of us who have been baptized into Christ Jesus were baptized into his death?*
> *4 Therefore we have been buried with him by baptism into death, so that, just as Christ was raised from the dead by the glory of the Father, so we too might walk in newness of life.*
> *5 For if we have united with him in a death like his, we will certainly be united with him in a resurrection like his.*
> *6 We know that our old self was crucified with him so that the body of sin might be destroyed, and we might no longer be enslaved to sin.*
> *7 For whoever has died is freed from sin.*
> *8 But if we have died with Christ, we believe that we will also live with him.*
> *9 We know that Christ, being raised from the dead, will never die again; death no longer has dominion over him.*
> *10 The death he died, he died to sin, once for all; but the life he lives, he lives to God.*
> *11 So you also must consider yourselves dead to sin and alive to God in Christ Jesus.*
> *12 Therefore, do not let sin exercise dominion in your mortal bodies, to make you obey their passions.*
> *13 No longer present your members to sin as instruments of*

> *wickedness, but present yourselves to God as instruments of righteousness.*
> *14 For sin will have no dominion over you, since you are not under law but under grace.*

God forgives sins. God's goodness triumphs. God justifies the sinner. The greatest gift God has given us is Jesus Christ, his Son and our Lord. God's grace is more abundant and stronger than our transgressions. Justification occurs out of utter goodness and grace. Faith is the only condition. From such a comforting truth may and should one not draw the conclusion that sin increases God's grace? Should one then not boldly state: the more sin, the more grace? Shall we not therefore persist in sin and dissolutely transgress God's commands?

Continue in sin in order that grace may abound! According to Paul, this is absurd. That idea — a suspicion, an accusation? — fills Paul with disgust. He reminds his readers of their baptism. Whoever is baptized has died to sin, is set free from sin. Such a person is no longer under the dominion of evil. The baptized person lives from grace, this excludes a life in sin. These two, grace and sin, are incompatible. By baptism we have become a new creation: dead to sin, alive to God. A radical split, a separation has taken place.

For Paul there is no mistaking that baptism can accomplish this separation only because of what happened on the cross. We are baptized into Christ Jesus. With him we have been buried into his death. Through baptism Christ appropriates the Christian. We must think of incorporation into Christ. This unification with Christ is basically effected through his death on the cross. It is pure grace. Because of Christ's blood it is costly grace. God's action, that is, God's active goodness in and through Christ, precedes our faith and baptism.

Christ has died and has been buried, but through God's power he has been raised from the dead. Does this resurrection also apply to us who have been buried with him into his death? No. Paul interrupts his comparison of the Christian with Christ. He switches from the past tense (see vv. 3-4a: "have been baptized; have been buried") to a purpose clause, and in v. 4b, instead of speaking of our resurrection, he points to a new type of behavior: "so (= in order) that ... we ... might walk in newness of life" (see also v. 8b: "we shall live"). Our resurrection lies in the future, and the quality of this future depends on the moral life that we as baptized people must live.

In this text, we recognize the distinction which Paul also elsewhere makes between the "indicative" of already given, present grace and the "imperative" of a new, Christian way of life. The gift brings with it the commitment to follow Christ. In this connection one can also speak of the Pauline "reservation": the Christian should not become triumphalistic, not rejoice prematurely. The battle is not yet completely fought; the outcome is not completely secure. The moral-religious behavior of the Christian requires daily effort. Its fruits will be decisive on the day of judgment. Since we live by the Spirit, we must also live according to the Spirit. We should not misuse the freedom to which we have been called as an opportunity for self-indulgence. On the contrary, we must serve one another in love (see Gal 5:13-25).

Are We to Sin? (Romans 6:15-7:6)

In Romans 6:15-7:6 Paul once more answers the disturbing, alarming question whether his view does not provide Christians with a license to continue sinning.

6:15 What then? Should we sin because we are not under law but under grace? By no means!
16 Do you not know that if you present yourselves to anyone as obedient slaves, you are slaves of the one whom you obey, either of sin, which leads to death, or of obedience, which leads to righteousness?
17 But thanks be to God that you, having once been slaves of sin, have become obedient from the heart to the form of teaching to which you were entrusted,
18 and that you, having been set free from sin, have become slaves of righteousness.
19 I am speaking in human terms because of your natural limitations. For just as you once presented your members as slaves to impurity and to greater and greater iniquity, so now present your members as slaves to righteousness for sanctification.
20 When you were slaves of sin, you were free in regard to righteousness.
21 So what advantage did you then get from the things of which you now are ashamed? The end of those things is death.
22 But now that you have been freed from sin and enslaved to God, the advantage you get is sanctification. The end is eternal life.
23 For the wages of sin is death, but the free gift of God is eternal life in Christ Jesus our Lord.
7:1 Do you not know, brothers and sisters — for I am speaking to those who know the law — that the law is binding on a person only during that person's lifetime?
2 Thus a married woman is bound by the law to her husband as long as he lives; but if her husband dies, she is discharged from the law concerning the husband.
3 Accordingly, she will be called an adulteress if she lives with another man while her husband is alive. But if her husband dies, she is free from that law, and if she marries another man, she is not an adulteress.
4 In the same way, my friends, you have died to the law through the body of Christ, so that you may belong to another, to him who has been raised from the dead in order that we may bear fruit for God.

> 5 *While we were living in the flesh, our sinful passions, aroused by the law, were at work in our members to bear fruit for death.*
> 6 *But now we are discharged from the law, dead to that which held us captive, so that we are slaves not under the old written code but in the new life of the Spirit.*

The content of 6:15b hardly differs from that of 6:1b. What is said about the law (5:20b and 6:14b) provokes the same objection. Does Paul's doctrine not lead to moral indifference, to sinful behavior?

In 6:15-7:6 two ways of being a slave are repeatedly opposed. Liberation brings a person from one dominion to the other. Liberation is a transition from a first enslaved situation to a second. Enslavement, as well as exercising dominion, were already mentioned in 6:1-14. Through the contrast of the two ways of being a slave, however, the new passage differs from the preceding one. This opposition is worked out in 6:16-23. Then, in 7:1-6, it is illustrated by means of an example.

The example of 7:1-6 is part of the answer to the question of 6:15. In it, Paul deepens somewhat his illustration of what it means to be set free from the law (6:14-15). The comparison with the married woman remains somewhat strange for us, and its application is not perfectly logical. Over and against the woman we have Christians, over and against the husband the law, and over and against the second man the risen Christ. In both cases liberation occurs through death. In the example, however, it is the husband who dies (7:2-3), while in the application (v. 4) it is not the law but Christians who die together with Jesus. "To belong to another, to him who has been raised from the dead" concretely requires "to bear fruit for God" (v. 4) through a life without sin.

Just as in 6:1-14 there is also, in 6:15-7:6, a tension between what is called the "indicative" and the "imperative," and between present and future. Death to sin is depicted as a fact which has already occurred (indicative), but the whole discourse is an exhortation to live from now on and in the future a sinless life (imperative). It is worth while following Paul's train of thought more closely.

In 6:16-20 Paul points to a contradiction between "being" and "living" which one must avoid. The principle is indicated: we are slaves of the one whom we obey. Obeying sin, therefore, would mean that we are and remain slaves of sin. Yet, we are set free from sin and have become slaves of righteousness. We must walk thus in newness of life, or even better, justification requires that we present our members as slaves to righteousness and so arrive at sanctification and holiness. Just as in 6:1-14, Paul reasons by means of the radical change which has taken place in baptism. We can call this the *sacramental* motivation.

In verses 21-23 the results of being a slave to sin are opposed to those of being a slave to righteousness. On the one hand there is impurity and "things we are now ashamed of"; the end is death. On the other hand, freedom from sin even now provides the possibility for a moral life which leads to holiness; the end is eternal life. That double perspective on the future — death for the sinner and eternal life for the one "enslaved to God" — possesses a warning and exhortative character. Besides the sacramental grounding, this text unit has also an *eschatological* motivation.

Just as in 6:3-11, so also in 7:4 the possibility of bearing fruit for God is connected with dying in Jesus Christ. We belong to "another," to Christ who has died and has been raised from the dead, because through his body we have died to the law (v. 4). In Romans 6 Paul has strongly emphasized our union with Christ. Our old self is crucified with him. By baptism we have been buried with him. True, we are not yet risen with him, but our future certainly lies in such a resurrection and, therefore, we must walk in newness of life. The sacramental argumentation is thus grounded in the Christ event. We must speak here of a third motivation which is undoubtedly *christological*.

In all three motivations the opposition between the verbs plays a major role. Sinful existence in the past is opposed to the time after the liberation, that is, the present of being a slave of righteousness together with the eschatological future. The intersection on this time line is Jesus' death and resurrection. What took place then and there is appropriated by the Christian in baptism.

II. THE LAW WHICH CAME LATER

For the time being one basic fact remains rather mysterious. Christians are no longer "under law" (6:14). They have died to the law (7:4); they are discharged from the law (7:6), they are freed from the law (see 7:1-3). Yet 6:16-23 speaks only of being a slave of sin, not of being a slave of the law. What is then the connection between law and sin? Although Paul alludes to the role of the law in 5:20, and once more in 7:5 (the role of law in regard to sin) it is only in 7:7-25 that he clearly formulates this question as a new objection and proceeds to answer it.

Earlier in this letter Paul explained the functions of the law. In Romans 1-7 we can distinguish three such functions.

The Law Brings Knowledge of Sin

In Romans 3:19-20 Paul concludes his discourse on the sinfulness of all human beings as follows:

> *Now we know that whatever the law says, it speaks to those who are under the law, so that every mouth may be silenced, and the whole world may be held accountable to God. For "no human being will be justified in his sight" by deeds prescribed by the law, for through the law comes the knowledge of sin.*

Paul's way of reasoning here is understandable. Even though one tries to observe the law, in the final analysis this proves to be impossible. Paul is convinced of the general sinfulness of humanity: "All have sinned and fall short of the glory of God" (3:23). The first function of the law is that of awakening the consciousness of sin. The requirements of the law inform us; through the law we know what sin is. All who transgress the law know that they sin and are guilty before God.

Transgression of the Law Calls for Punishment

In Romans 4 Paul opposes promises and law, God's original promise to Abraham and the Sinai law which came later. That promise says that Abraham and his offspring will inherit the world. The promise does not depend on the law; it is not given to Abraham because he kept the law. No, Abraham believed God, and this was reckoned to him as righteousness. We, too, must not desire to obtain the promise by observing the law. "For the law brings wrath; but where there is no law, neither is there violation" (4:15).

The law not only brings knowledge of sin, the law also requires that the transgression of its prescriptions be punished. If there were no law, there would be no transgression.

According to Paul, a second function of the law is that lawbreaking produces God's wrath and punishment.

The Law Arouses Sinful Desires

In Romans 5:13 we read that "sin is not reckoned when there is no law." In 5:12-14 Paul reflects on the period of time between Adam and Moses. Before the law, "sin was indeed in the world." Within this period, however, people did not sin in the way Adam had sinned, that is, through transgression of an explicit commandment.

The law came later and through it transgressions were multiplied. According to Paul, through the Sinai law sin has increased; sin "exercised dominion in death" (see 5:20-21).

Paul insists that the law arouses sinful passions in us (see 7:5). This is the third and most tragic function of the law. The law increases sin; law-breaking is repeated; by the law the sinful passions are invoked.

III. SIN AND THE LAW IN CURRENT EXEGESIS

It would seem that many modern readers sympathize with Paul's opponents. When Paul repeatedly emphasizes that human faithlessness cannot undo God's faithfulness (Romans 3:3), that God justifies the ungodly who without "works" believes him (4:5), that no human being is justified in the sight of God by keeping the law (3:20), and that God's righteousness is effective through faith in Christ for all who believe, without distinction (3:21-23), then today's readers can to a certain extent be in sympathy with the defenders of opposite views in long-ago days.

Sin

The problem of the opponents is not only Paul's view of justification. They must have especially feared that his doctrine would open the floodgates for sin. The more sin, all the more grace! Let us do what is wrong so that good may come out of it! One can continue in sin, can repeat it, for God's good abounds through such a human behavior! Paul has problems with these kinds of conclusions. As we have seen, he must put them down over and over again.

Christians today will easily admit that Paul could not have been favorably disposed towards sin. Yet, is the way Paul sees the law and its relation to sin acceptable?

The Law

Many modern readers, almost spontaneously, also protest against what Paul says about the law. True, Paul holds that "the law and the prophets" bear witness to the righteousness which God brings in Jesus Christ (3:21). Paul equally maintains that his view does not undermine nor overthrow the law, it upholds it (3:31). Yet, according to Paul, righteousness has been disclosed "apart from the law" (3:21), without works done in obedience to the law. The law thus has nothing to do with justification. One is not justified by keeping the law (3:20). Readers, however, ask: Why not? All this sounds quite so strange!

All of us easily see that through the law there is knowledge and consciousness of sin. All of us understand and agree that transgressors of the law commit sin and will be punished by God. Without much difficulty we can also admit that sin may corrupt the law; sin "uses" the law in the sense that the law transforms the evil deed into a transgression of an explicit commandment. Thus the sinfulness of sin increases. Moreover, the law often arouses sinful passions in us. By common human experience we realize that a forbidden fruit possesses its attraction. All this is quite understandable.

What must we think of the Lutheran thesis that the human being is innerly so perverted that everything done without grace is sinful? According to this view the powerlessness of the law lies on a deeper level than the act of transgression. The law can never justify, even if it were to be kept completely. For, by trying to observe the law, Jews seek their own righteousness. Therefore, the works of the law are always deficient. Self-righteousness through works is never able to attain God's righteousness. Human activity is affected to its roots. Since sin has dominion over the deepest kernel of the human being, both observing and transgressing the law, good works as well as evil deeds, always express and concretize sin. The "holy" law is radically perverted by sin. One must further bear in mind: "seeking to establish one's own righteousness" (10:3) is characteristic not only of the Jews of Paul's days. No, such a legalistic drive is at work in each human being.

A great number of exegetes, however, have become convinced that Paul, both in Romans and Galatians, is not primarily dealing with the Lutheran (anthropological) question, "How do I find righteousness in God's sight?" Paul is more concerned with what could be called a socio-ecclesiastical problem, "Under what conditions can Gentiles become Christians?" Paul is not giving in to introspection. He does not primarily fight against works-righteousness. He protests against the view that Gentile Christians must live as Jews (see Galatians 2:11-14). Paul maintains that Gentiles have a direct access to righteousness, apart from the Jewish works of the law, through faith in Jesus Christ. For Jews, therefore, there is no longer boasting. Since a person is justified by faith, not by keeping the law, it is manifest that God is not only the God of Jews but also the God of Gentiles (see Rom 3:27-30).

This new approach, of course, does not solve all our problems. What is the precise meaning of the expression "works of the law"? It would seem that Paul does not reject the whole law. In more than one passage of his letter he speaks of the fulfillment of the law (through love), and in Romans 3:31 he even claims that he "is upholding" the law. In these and similar passages, however, Paul can hardly include in that fulfillment of the law circumcision and food regulations. Further, a human being is not justified by keeping the law; justification comes only by faith. Yet after justification Christians must keep the law, at least the moral requirements of the law. How are we to interpret Paul's often rather confusing language?

In Romans 7 and 8 Paul does not provide us with a totally satisfactory answer to these many questions. Yet it is worth analyzing what these chapters say about sin and grace, about the sinful "I" which is sold into slavery under sin, and about the wonder of God's redemption with its cosmic implications, as well as the Christian conviction of salvation.

CHAPTER TWO

Romans 7:7-25:
Its Structure and Line of Thought

The study of Romans 7 requires a first attentive reading of the text which mainly focuses on its structure and line of thought. The New Revised Standard Version runs as follows:

7a What then should we say?
 b That the law is sin?
 c By no means!
 d Yet, if it had not been for the law, I would not have known sin.
 e I would not have known what it is to covet if the law had not said, "You shall not covet" (Exodus 20:17 and Deuteronomy 5:21).
8a But sin, seizing an opportunity in the commandment, produced in me all kinds of covetousness.
 b Apart from the law sin lies dead.
9a I was once alive apart from the law,
 b but when the commandment came, sin revived
10a and I died,
 b and the very commandment that promised life proved to be death to me.
11 For sin, seizing an opportunity in the commandment, deceived me and through it killed me.
12a So the law is holy,
 b and the commandment is holy and just and good ....
13a Did what is good, then, bring death to me?
 b By no means!
 c It was sin, working death in me through what is good, in order that sin might be shown to be sin,

d and through the commandment might become sinful beyond measure.
14a For we know that the law is spiritual;
  b but I am of the flesh, sold into slavery under sin.
15a I do not understand my own actions.
  b For I do not do what I want,
  c but I do the very thing I hate.
16a Now if I do what I do not want,
  b I agree that the law is good.
17a But in fact it is no longer I that do it,
  b but sin that dwells within me.
18a For I know that nothing good dwells within me, that is, in my flesh.
  b I can will what is right, but I cannot do it.
19a For I do not do the good I want,
  b but the evil I do not want is what I do.
20a Now if I do what I do not want,
  b it is no longer I that do it, but sin that dwells within me.
21a So I find it to be a law that when I want to do what is good,
  b evil lies close at hand.
22 For I delight in the law of God in my inmost self,
23 but I see in my members another law at war with the law of my mind, making me captive to the law of sin that dwells in my members.
24a Wretched man that I am!
  b Who will rescue me from this body of death?
25a Thanks be to God through Jesus Christ our Lord!
  b So then, with my mind I am a slave to the law of God, but with my flesh I am a slave to the law of sin.

What immediately strikes the reader are the numerous repetitions and the language of its argumentation. Ten times Paul uses the explanatory or demonstrative particle *gar* ("for"). One gets the impression that Paul is struggling with his own ideas and that he wants to nuance them over and over again.

I. THE STRUCTURE

The text itself and its immediate context provide some data which will help us to detect the structure of Romans 7:7-25, as well as to follow Paul's train of thought in this passage.

The Diatribe Style

Verses 7 and 13 are characterized by brief questions and answers. Stylistically, they belong to what is called the "diatribe." We have already met this style in Paul, namely in Romans 3:1-8 and 6:1-2 and 15-16.

In regard to this style, it was once customary to refer immediately to the popular speech of religious orators or propagandists and wandering preachers. In addition to its simple and lively, frequently also its touching and pathetic tone, the main characteristic of the diatribe is the dialogue form. The speaker employs the second person, addressing a well-known figure or a fictitious person, often as if an adversary who is interrogated or who is allowed to raise objections were present in the audience. The speaker makes this person ask questions (which, it should be noted, the speaker actually formulates). The speaker answers those questions, sometimes by means of a counter-question. The speaker may feign astonishment or indignation, may reject the question and often becomes ironic and abusive. As a matter of fact, in the diatribe strict argumentation seldom occurs. There are few long, well-constructed periods. For the most part, there are only short sentences. Instead of conclusive argumentation, personal attack predominates. The opponent is silenced, often ridiculed. The style is a mixture of seriousness and humor. This way of speaking is nervous, quick and very fast-moving with ideas and motifs, comparisons and antitheses. The diatribe is above all chosen for rhetorical effect.

New studies have demonstrated that this style was also used in philosophical schools. The opposition there is not speaker-opponent, but teacher-disciple. The dialogue form functions as a didactic means, a rhetorical technique and strategy. The teacher wants to preserve the disciple from error, to bring the student to truth and wisdom. The originally spoken style was often taken over and imitated in written texts.

The influence of the diatribe style on Paul, especially in Romans, seems to be beyond question, Rudolf Bultmann has shown. Yet, Bultmann warns us that Paul uses other forms of expressions as well and that he remains original: Paul modifies, qualifies and even transforms borrowed elements.

Notwithstanding Paul's freedom and variation, one can see a basic pattern. We often find a double question and a double answer:

– First (a) a short question, followed by (b) a second, longer question which as it were provides a "filling" to the first.

– Then comes (c) the first short answer, often no more than an emotional outcry, followed by (d) the second explanatory answer which is sometimes put in question form.

Romans 6:1-2 presents a good example:

> *(a) What then are we to say?*
> *(b) Should we continue in sin in order that grace may abound?*
> *(c) By no means!*
> *(d) How can we who died to sin go on living in it?*

In Romans 7:7 we also find the four elements:

(a) What then should we say?
(b) That the law is sin?
(c) By no means!
(d) Yet, if it had not been for the law, I would not have known sin. I would not have known what it is to covet if the law had not said, "You shall not covet."

In 7:13 only elements (b), (c) and (d) are present:

(b) Did what is good, then, bring death to me?
(c) By no means!
(d) It was sin, working death in me through what is good, in order that sin might be shown to be sin, and through the commandment might become sinful beyond measure.

The Inclusion (Romans 7:6 and 8:2)

The "inclusion" is a figure of speech which is often used by biblical authors. By means of an inclusion a speaker or writer "frames" a text. Words and ideas from the beginning are repeated at the end; in this way the text unit is "included." We may perhaps consider Romans 7:6 and 8:2 as an inclusion in regard to 7:7-25.

We can safely hold that 7:7, leaving aside verse 6, refers back to 7:5. There, in verse 5, it was said that our sinful desires were stirred up by the law. Does this mean that the law itself is sin (see 7:7)? The rest of chapter 7 is used by Paul in order to refute this erroneous conclusion. Willem Grossouw comments: "One can say that 7:7-25 is exactly a drastic working out of 7:5 ... All the elements of the unregenerate condition (flesh, sin, passion, law, members, death) will recur in 7:7-25" (p. 71).

Romans 7:6 stands opposite 7:5. The expression *nyni de* ("but now") emphasizes the start of a new historical period. The time of being in the flesh, of the dominion of sin and of captivity, has come to an end. It is now possible to live according to the Spirit.

The temporal adverb *nyn* is also present in 8:1. Yet, it is rather with 8:2 that 7:6 constitutes an inclusion. We should compare:

> 7:6 *But now we are discharged from the law, dead to that which held us captive, so that we are slaves not under the old written code but in the new life of the Spirit,*

with

> 8:2 *For the law of the Spirit of life in Christ Jesus has set you free from the law of sin and of death.*

Where 7:6 speaks of "being discharged from the law, dead to that which held us captive," 8:2 mentions a liberation "from the law of sin and death." Both verses deal with law and death, with the Spirit and new life. They form an inclusion. Between these two framing verses Romans 7:7-25 discusses the time and the human condition *before* the deliverance.

An Interruption in the Text (Romans 7:12 and 13)

It appears that the sentence in 7:12 has been broken off and remains unfinished. It would seem that verse 12 is meant as a conclusion: "So, on the one hand (= the Greek particle *men*), the law [is] holy, and the commandment holy and just and good ...." But this conclusion is incomplete. We have only its first half (the *men* clause) which, as a matter of fact, does not follow from what precedes. We rather expect a statement about the disastrous activity of sin. The present verse is more or less concessive and points to a generally admitted truth: "It is true and everybody agrees (= the meaning of *men*) that the law is holy, and the commandment holy, just and good." Originally, Paul must have planned a second clause (introduced by the Greek particle *de*: "on the other hand"), more or less as follows regarding content: "but sin has misused this holy law and this good commandment" (see the end of v. 13c).

That second clause, however, is absent. In verse 13 Paul begins with another question: "Did what is good, then, bring death to me?" The question shows that Paul continues to have in mind the good commandment. Without completing verse 12 he immediately formulates the obvious objection. We have thus a certain interruption, a caesura in the train of thought. Although verse 13a asks a question which arises from what is developed in verses 7-12, the verse constitutes a new start.

This is confirmed by the diatribe style in verse 13. That style with question-and-answer often introduces a new pericope (see, for instance, 6:1-2 and 6:15-16).

There is, however, yet another item. Although in the whole text unit of verses 7d-25 the "I" is speaking, a shift occurs between verse 12 and verse 13. In verses 7-12, what happened in the past is described. The verbs are put in a past tense. This is still the case in verse 13, but in verses 14-25 most of the verbs are in the present tense. The "I" now depicts an enduring situation which is the result of what has occurred in the past.

In view of all these considerations — except the last one — it seems to me better not to add verse 13 to the first part, but to consider it as an introduction to the second.

The End of the Pericope (Romans 7:24-8:1)

In 7:24-8:1 five small units can be distinguished.
(1) There is the outcry of *7:24a*: "Wretched man that I am!" The theological exposition is disrupted by this per-

sonal plaintive reaction. Paul was obviously emotionally involved in his own description.

(2) Then the question of *7:24b* is raised: "Who will rescue me from this body of death?" This question is an existential call for help.

(3) Because of its shortness, *7,25a*, "Thanks be to God through Jesus Christ our Lord," is somewhat enigmatic. Is it a thanksgiving which, as such, presupposes an unexpressed answer to the previous question? Or, as is more likely, is Paul actually giving this answer: deliverance has taken place through Christ, thanks be to God?

(4) The first three elements are more or less interjections; emotion has played its role. But with *7:25b* Paul returns to the exposition of 7:7-23. "So then, with my mind I am a slave to the law of God, but with my flesh I am a slave to the law of sin." This verse is a summary of and, at the same time, draws the conclusion (see the two consecutive particles *ara* and *oun*, "thus" and "therefore") to the whole preceding paragraph.

(5) Paul, however, did not forget the question of 7:24b. Thus he writes now in a more sober manner in *8:1*: "There is therefore now no condemnation for those who are in Christ Jesus." From here on he will be dealing with the new Christian state, "life in Christ" (see 8:2) and "being in the Spirit" (see 8:9).

Romans 7:24-8:1 is certainly a transition passage. On the one hand, with 7:24a and 25b Paul still remains close to the description of 7:7-23. On the other hand, in 7:24b the question of deliverance is raised. The thanksgiving of 7:25a is, or supposes, an answer to this question. From 8:1 onwards the new life in the Spirit is the subject matter of what follows.

This rather complex whole of transitional verses must not

prevent us from considering 7:7-25 as consisting of two sections: a mainly narrative part, verses 7-12, and a mainly descriptive part, verses 13-25. The ensuing analysis of the line of thought must take into account this twofold structure.

II. THE LINE OF THOUGHT

Between the first section of Romans 7:7-25 and the second there are many connections of content. Moreover, the use of "I" in the two sections causes the entire pericope to remain a tightly unified whole.

The First Part (Romans 7:7-12)

The objection in verse 7ab asks whether the law is sin. The concrete reason for this question is verse 5 from the preceding pericope. There Paul writes that when "flesh" exercised its dominion over our existence, the law aroused sinful desires within us and that these desires were at work in our members. Is the law with such a function not sin? In verse 7c Paul answers negatively: *mê genoito* ("by no means!"). More emphatically, at the end of this first part the concluding (and concessive) verse 12 declares that the law is holy, and the commandment holy, just and good. The repetition in this verse 12, as well as the symmetry between law and commandment, and the three adjectives "holy, just and good" must manifest Paul's deepest conviction. His ideas should not be misunderstood.

In verse 7d the "I"-style commences and, at the same time, the answer: "Yet, if it had not been for the law, I would not have known sin." What follows, up to and including verse 11, will clarify this answer. First, in verse 7e, it is stated once more that there would not have been knowledge of sin (or of sinful desire) without the law. The law is cited: "You shall not covet." Then, in verse 8, it is argued positively that sin took the opportunity to stir up wrong desires, "all kinds of covetousness," in me by means of the commandment. This tragedy is worked out in verses 9-10: how I formerly lived without the law, and sin, though present, was "dead" (v. 8b); how sin started to live when the commandment came; and how I died because of this. The very commandment which promised life brought death to me! Verse 11 repeats in one sentence the whole of verses 8-10: sin found its opportunity and through the commandment seduced me; sin, by means of the commandment, thus killed me.

Perhaps we may propose for Romans 7:7-12 the following structure:
(1) Verses 7-8 contain the objection and provide the reader with an already extensive answer;
(2) verses 9-11 clarify the answer;
(3) verse 12 concludes the first part.

The Second Part (Romans 7:13-25)

The question of verse 13a raises a new objection. The last word of verse 12 is taken up: "good." Did what is *good* bring about death? Once more the answer is a definite no (v. 12b: "by no means!"). Verse 13c repeats what has been said before: It is sin that worked death in me by using what is good. The sinfulness of sin is explicitly underscored. In verses 14-23 a point will be dealt with which up till now has been only asserted: the presence of sin in the "I" and its divisive consequences.

While the first part (vv. 7-12), by showing what happened when the commandment came, narrated a story, a sequence of events, the second part (vv. 13-25) directs attention to a remaining situation in the "I": the dominion of sin and what kind of disorder this brought about in the "I." Human, personal experience is called upon: see *oidamen* (v. 14: "we know"); *oida* (v. 18: "I know"); *heuriskô* (v. 21: "I find"); *blepô* (v. 23: "I see").

After verse 13, the statement of verse 14 is clear: The law is spiritual. In a confessional mood Paul adds: but I am carnal, sold under sin.

In verses 15-20 is shown what the presence of sin brought about in me: disunity and a hopeless opposition between will and action. The description is full of repetition — Paul wrestles to find the right wording. The will to do good is present, but the possibility of performing it is absent. I do the very thing I hate. So I am not really the one who does this thing but it is the sin that lives in me. Yet, Paul does not in the least exculpate the "I." Its full responsibility remains.

Almost unnoticeably a shift has taken place. Verses 15-16 deal with the "I" itself. In verse 17-20, however, Paul distinguishes between the "I" and the sin which is within the "I" and works in it. Verses 17 and 20b form an inclusion for this group of verses. Compare verse 17:

But in fact it is no longer I that do it, but sin that dwells within me

with verse 20b

it is no longer I that do it, but sin that dwells within me.

Finally, verses 21-23 and 25 formulate the diagnosis which results from all these sincere confessions. I find, Paul says, that I want to do what is good, but that only the wrong is within my reach; there is within me another law that fights against the law of my mind and makes me captive to the law of sin. This brings Paul to the outcry, "Wretched man that I am!" (v. 24a). Immediately afterwards Paul's thanksgiving points to the liberation of the "I" (v. 24b).

We are thus brought to distinguish in Paul's line of thought four small units:
(1) Verses 13-14: the fleshly "I;"
(2) verses 15-20: the conflict situation in the "I;"
(3) verses 21-23: the diagnosis;
(4) verses 24-25: misery and liberation of the "I."

III. Remarks and Questions

Notwithstanding our analysis of structure and line of thought the first reading of Romans 7:7-25 leaves us with an undefinable feeling and a somewhat contradictory impression.

Text and Context

What is narrated in the first part has a rather mythological character. Sin is presented as a living person. Sin uses, or better, misuses the law. Sin kills the "I." How can we understand this?

Paul forcefully defends the holiness of the law; with equal emphasis he maintains in verse 13 that "through what is good" (i.e., the law) sin has brought about the death of the "I." That is the beginning of the second part. The law is, of course, spiritual. But "I" am fleshly, carnal, sold as a slave under sin. Once again, how must we interpret all this?

In 7:7-12 everything is strange and tragically negative. Then, in 7:13-25, comes a moving passage about the hopeless situation of the "I" and its moral powerlessness. Each of us recognizes in this description a dimension of his or her existence. The second part of the pericope is true to life and in all its tragedy movingly sad. At the end, for just one moment in 7:24b-25a, redemption from that wretched condition is alluded to.

The investigation of the structure and the line of thought in Romans 7:7-25 has convinced us of its adequate place in the letter's context. As elsewhere in Romans, in 7:7 and 13 Paul uses questions and answers in diatribe style. We have seen that, with regard to its content, the passage is dependent on 7:5. In our passage 7:5 is worked out and explained. Furthermore, the transition to the following subject, the redemption and the new life in Christ, begins in the pericope, namely, in 7:24b-25a. Moreover, the themes of sin and law are the continuation of what is dealt with in 6:1-14 and 6:15-7:6. For after these two passages, wherein the question whether the Christians who are set free from the law may continue in sin is asked and answered, the reader expects an answer to the other question of 7:7ab concerning the law: is the law sin? This is the subject matter of the following section, 7:7cde-25. The negative answer to this question will thoroughly reflect on the way sin misuses the law and on the consequences for the "I" of its being sold into slavery under sin.

The "I"

The great surprise in Romans 7:7-25 is Paul's use of the first person singular. In 6:15-7:6 Paul speaks to the Roman Christians in the second person plural. In 7:1 and 4 he addresses them as "brothers and sisters" (*adelphoi*); the plural "you" and "your" occurs frequently in the whole passage. The inclusive plural "we" and "our" appears at two places: in 6:15 Paul begins the pericope with the inclusive plural and in 7:4-6 he concludes that same passage using again the first person plural. So the shift to the first person singular, to "I," in the midst of 7:7 is completely unexpected. In 7:14, there is one more plural, almost an accidental one: *oidamen* ("we know"). Throughout the unit, however, the first person singular is really dominant.

The "I" of Romans 7:7-25 raises a twofold question. The first and obvious question is whether Paul here writes autobiographically or, more precisely, purely autobiographically. The second question concerns the times and time periods in this pericope. It is not immediately evident to the reader when the "I" was living (v. 9a), when the commandment had been given and sin came to life (v. 9b), when sin had deceived the "I" and brought about its death (vv. 10-11). Thus the reader does not clearly see in what time period the hopeless condition which is depicted in verses 14-25 has to be placed.

We must therefore try to find an answer to these two questions. First, however, let us return to the text itself for a second reading. A number of details require a more thorough treatment and a more accurate exegesis.

CHAPTER THREE

Romans 7:7-25: Exegesis

A fair number of details in Romans 7:7-25 merit our special attention. While seeking the background of expressions and looking for the more or less hidden allusions to the Old Testament, data will appear which may prove to be important in determining the identity of the "I" and situating what is said about the "I" within the correct period of time. We will therefore gather together various bits of information. In the meantime we postpone the explicit discussion of the "I." This third chapter is still preparatory work.

I. THE FIRST PART (Romans 7:7-12)

The investigation of the first part can be divided into three short paragraphs, first verses 7-8, then verses 9-11 and finally verse 12 (see p. 37-38).

Sin and the Law (vv. 7-8)

7a What then should we say?
b That the law is sin?
c By no means!
d Yet, if it had not been for the law, I would not have known sin.
e I would not have known what it is to covet if the law had not

> said, "You shall not covet" (Exodus 20:17 and Deuteronomy 5:21).
> 8a But sin, seizing an opportunity in the commandment, produced in me all kinds of covetousness.
> b Apart from the law sin lies dead.

The question is asked: are the law and sin the same thing? The opposing "yet" in verse 7d follows the emotional negation *mê genoito* ("by no means, certainly not, of course not"). This radical, clear answer of verse 7c does not provide an explanation and is, therefore, not sufficient. What we find in verse 7d must complement that lacuna and, at the same time, nuance the answer. A paraphrasing translation may indicate Paul's intention and his concessive tone: "Yet, *it is true*, if it had not been for the law, I would not have known sin." The law thus has something to do with sin.

The NRSV translates *egnôn* of verse 7d and *êdein* of verse 7e by the same English verb "to know." Both Greek verbs refer here to experiential knowledge, not to mere intellectual insight, but it should be noted that the tenses are different. "If it had not been for the law, I would not have known" (v. 7d) contains a past condition contrary to fact. A more correct translation of verse 7e reads: "I *would not know* what it is to covet if the law *did not say* ..."; the sentence contains a present condition contrary to fact. The "learning" (v. 7d) is past; the resulting "knowing" (v. 7e) is still present and remains.

The citation in verse 7e, "You shall not covet," just as that in Romans 13:9, gives only the beginning of the text of Exodus 20:17 (see also Deuteronomy 5:21). In the Old Testament text the verb possesses more than one object: "You shall not covet your neighbor's house; you shall not covet your neigbor's wife, or male or female slave, or ox, or donkey, or anything that belongs to your neighbor." Does Paul, notwithstanding this abbreviation, refer to the so-called tenth "commandment"? It is often said that Paul, by quoting but two words (*ouk epithymêseis*), wants to keep the commandment general (see in v. 8: *pasan epithymian*, "all kinds of covetousness"). At the same time, with the verb "covet," Paul would want to direct the reader's attention to the inner reality, that is, to the origin of sin within the human heart. For Jewish tradition teaches that desire is the beginning of all sin. In chapter five of our book (see p. 77), we shall criticize this opinion as far as the generalization is concerned.

It is not to be excluded *a priori* that the Old Testament citation together with verse 8 (and also verses 9-11) must be understood against a specific Jewish background. According to rabbinical tradition Jews are obliged to observe the commandments of the law only after having experienced the first signs of manhood. Only at the age of puberty did the Jewish boy become *barmitzvah*, "Son of the Commandment." Does Paul, using "I," reflect upon his own youth, upon the sexual drive which in reaching manhood increased in intensity? Or did he transpose this background and apply it to another event either in himself or in Israel?

The opportunity which sin seizes is the proclamation of the law. The expression *dia tês entolês* in verse 8a ("by means of the commandment," that is a concrete prescription of the law) can, abstractly speaking, qualify either the preceding verb ("to seize," in participle form) or the main verb *katergazomai* ("to produce") which follows the expression, or each of the two verbs. There is a similar uncertainty in verse 11. In verse 13c, however, the expression "through what is good" certainly qualifies only the verb *katergazomai* ("to work", here in participle form) which likewise comes after the phrase. The order of the words in the three verses, together with the presence of the same Greek verb in verse 13c and verse 8a, seems to indicate that for verses 8a and 11 the second possibility is to be preferred (otherwise in the NRSV). The commandment is for the sin a means, an instrument, more than an opportunity to be seized.

"Apart from the law sin lies dead" (v. 8b). Sin is present, but like a sleeping serpent sin seems to be a dead thing. Is sin completely idle? Hardly. In Romans 5:12-13 we read:

> *12 Therefore, just as sin came into the world through one man, and death came through sin, and so death spread to all because all have sinned — 13 sin was indeed in the world before the law, but sin is not reckoned when there is no law.*

What Paul writes in Romans 7:8b contains the same idea as in 5:13b: apart from the law sin is dead; apart from the law sin is not reckoned. Yet during that period of time people were sinning since "death exercised dominion from Adam to Moses, even over those whose sins were not like the transgression of Adam" (5:14ab). This raises the question whether the "I" of Romans 7 represents all human beings between Adam and Moses.

The Tragic Event (vv. 9-11)

9a I was once alive apart from the law,
  b but when the commandment came, sin revived
10a and I died,
  b and the very commandment that promised life proved to be death to me.
11 For sin, seizing an opportunity in the commandment, deceived me and through it killed me.

In verse 9a the personal pronoun *egô* appears for the first time. In Romans 7:7-25 it occurs ten times, three times as *egô de* ("but I") in verses 9a, 10a and 14b and once as *autos egô* ("I myself" or "I by, of myself") in verse 25b.

It is well known that the wording of Romans 5:12 is influenced by Wisdom 2:24a: "But through the devil's envy death entered the world." The Wisdom passage itself is already an interpretation of Genesis 3. The serpent is identified with the devil. Paul, in his turn, interprets Wisdom. In Romans 5:12 he writes: "Through one man sin came into the world, and death came through sin ...." Neither devil nor serpent is mentioned. Romans 7:11 is most probably dependent on Genesis 3:13 which reads: "The serpent deceived me." For "deceived" Genesis has *epatêsen*, Paul in Romans 7:11 *exepatêsen* (see also 2 Cor 11:3: "the serpent deceived — *exepatêsen* — Eve"). In Romans 7:11, just as in 5:12, "sin" takes the place of the devil. This is a first factor.

In Genesis 3:1-5 we see how the serpent made use of the prohibition (see Gen 2:16-17) in order to seduce the woman. Sin does the same thing in Romans 7:8a and 11 (see also v. 13). We can accept without much risk that Paul here remembers the story of the Fall, just as he has already done in 5:12. The commandment which in Paradise was meant to protect the life of Adam and Eve brought death (see Gen 3:3: "or you shall die"). In Romans 7:10b Paul writes: "and the very commandment that promised life proved to be death to me." Is the "I" of Romans 7 perhaps the first man, Adam, rather than the human beings between Adam and Moses and also rather than Paul himself? There can be no doubt that verses 9-11 allude to what occurred in the Garden. Once Adam was alive; then came the commandment; the serpent misuses that commandment and seduces Eve; Adam transgresses God's commandment as well and both will die.

In 7:9b the NRSV translates: "but when the commandment came, sin *re*vived." The Greek verb *anazaô* originally meant "to live again, to return to life" (see this verb in Luke 15:24: "this son of mine was dead and is alive *again*"), but later, with neglect of *ana*, also in a weakened sense "to spring to life, to become alive." If Paul intends the first meaning, then he thinks of sin which entered the world through Adam and which has formerly been alive, namely during the Fall. Afterwards, while remaining present in a dormant condition, sin only *re*vived when the law was promulgated on mount Sinai (compare Rom 5:12-14 and 20). In this case "I" cannot be Adam! It can also be questioned whether that original strong meaning is still present?

The Conclusion (v. 12)

12a So the law is holy,
 b and the commandment is holy and just and good....

Verse 12 concludes the first part. Although sin misused the law in such a tragic way, the law itself is not sin. Originally the law has been intended for life (see v. 10b). The law and its commandments remain holy, just and good. The two clauses of verse 12 and the three adjectives of verse 12 which complete the first section emphasize Paul's deepest conviction. He defends the law: the law is the opposite of sin. So, by means of verse 12 he has clearly answered the question of verse 7b.

II. THE SECOND PART (Romans 7:13-25)

As we have seen, the problems of the first part are situated on the salvation historical level. To what event in the past does Paul make allusion? The difficulties of the second section are more anthropological. How does Paul see the innerly divided "I"? Of what precisely does the division in the "I" consist? Does Paul depict a past, no longer existing situation or is that situation in the Christian still a present reality? We will successively deal with the four small units which have been pointed out on p. 38-40.

The Fleshly "I" (vv. 13-14)

13a Did what is good, then, bring death to me?
b By no means!
c It was sin, working death in me through what is good, in order that sin might be shown to be sin,
d and through the commandment might become sinful beyond measure.
14a For we know that the law is spiritual;
b but I am of the flesh, sold into slavery under sin.

In the Greek, verse 10b ends with the phrase *eis thanaton* ("to death," opposed to *eis zôên*, "to life," in the same clause); verse 11 ends with the verb "to kill" and verse 12 with the adjective "good." In verse 13a Paul begins the second part with a new question which is, just as in verse 7, an erroneous conclusion. That question takes the vocabulary we have mentioned: "Did what is *good*, then, bring *death* to me?" No, by no means, is Paul's answer in verse 13b. Paul then repeats in verse 13c what he had already said in the first part: by means of what is good, that is, using the law, sin worked death in me. Through the transgression of the law sin shows its true nature and becomes sinful beyond measure (v. 13d; see also 5:20a: "law came in, with the result that the trespass multiplied"). In verse 13cd, besides the adjective "sinful," the noun "sin" occurs three times. Moreover, there are two purpose clauses (*hina*, "in order that") and two expressions with "by means of" (*dia* + genitive). Because of all this, verse 13cd is a lengthy and very ponderous sentence, indeed.

Paul emphasizes that the law, to be sure, is holy and the commandment holy, just and good (see v. 12). It is also true, he says in verse 14a, that the law is spiritual and as such it thus comes from God, from the Spirit of God. But, he adds immediately in verse 14b, "I am of the flesh, sold into slavery under sin."

With regard to the term *sarkinos* ("of the flesh, fleshly, carnal") two things must be kept in mind. (1) In the context of Romans 7 "to be fleshly" is the same as to be delivered to sin, to be under its dominion. "Fleshly" is not to be understood here in the rather neutral sense of creature-like dependence and fragility. In other contexts, some of which are in Paul, the term *sarx* ("flesh") can have this meaning, but in Romans 7 and 8 we do have the specific Pauline concept of moral weakness and sinfulness (in these two chapters, in addition to *sarkinos*, the noun *sarx* occurs no less than 16 times!) (2) The whole "I," the whole person is "fleshly," not solely the body or sensual desires.

What about the other anthropological concepts in this second part? In verse 23 Paul twice speaks of the "members" (*melê*) of the carnal "I." According to 7:5 the sinful desires are very active in the members and bear fruit for death. Paul undoubtedly means the members of the body. It must be noted that in Pauline anthropology "body" (*sôma*) and "member" usually do not coincide with "flesh." This is obvious, for example, in 1 Corinthians 15 where verse 50 states that "flesh and blood," that is "the perishable," cannot inherit the kingdom of God, while elsewhere in this chapter the resurrection of the "body" is stressed. See also Romans 8:11: the Spirit will give life to the "mortal body."

Yet it may happen that "body" (so, for example in Romans 8:13: "the deeds of the body") or "members" (so, for example in 7:23) have more or less the same pejorative meaning as is typical of Paul's "flesh."

The NRSV reads Romans 7:24b as follows: "Who will rescue me from this body of death?" A more literal translation would read: "Who will deliver me out of the body of this death?" The Semitic expression "the body of *this* death" can be the equivalent of "*this* body of the death." The body is perverted by sin and must therefore die. Here, too, the body is the whole person. Thus Paul asks: Who is going to rescue me from (*ek*) myself, from that sinful "I"? It would be wrong to interpret the preposition *ek* (literally: "out of") as a deliverance of the soul out of the body. This remark equally applies to Romans 8:23: "the redemption of our bodies" is not the abandonment of the bodies, but their liberation, concretely speaking: their resurrection.

Over and against the carnal "I," there is in verse 22 my "inmost self" (*esô anthrôpos*) and in verses 23 and 25 my "mind" (*nous*). At first sight this distinction possesses a dualistic ring. No more than "flesh" (and "body") do, however, do both "mind" and "inmost self" point to a part of the human person. By means of these two terms the whole person is meant insofar as this person (still) knows the law of God and (still) wants to live according that law (but is unable to do it). That person, however, is not yet the redeemed Christian. One should not deny that Paul here uses hellenistic terminology which, to be sure, he thoroughly adapts.

The Conflict Within the "I" (vv. 15-20)

15a   I do not understand my own actions.
b   For I do not do what I want,
c   but I do the very thing I hate.
16a   Now if I do what I do not want,
b   I agree that the law is good.
17a   But in fact it is no longer I that do it,
b   but sin that dwells within me.
18a   For I know that nothing good dwells within me, that is, in my flesh.
b   I can will what is right, but I cannot do it.
19a   For I do not do the good I want,
b   but the evil I do not want is what I do.
20a   Now if I do what I do not want,
b   it is no longer I that do it, but sin that dwells within me.

In 7:15-20 the experience of inner conflict and division is described. In verse 15a the direct object of "I do not know" (*ou ginôskô*, v. 15a) is "what I work" (*ho katergazomai*). We should interpret: I cannot see, I do not understand how I am brought to do the evil actions (see the NRSV). Rudolf Bultmann explains this incorrectly, I think, in a more radical sense. He paraphrases as follows: I do not know where my actions are leading (namely to death). In his opinion all that is done by the legalistic and carnal "I," even the observation of the law, is sinful; it always brings about death, for human nature is in its inner essence corrupted.

Reading verse 15bc, "For I do not do what I want, but I do the very thing I hate," we spontaneously think of the famous lines of Ovid: *Video meliora proboque, deteriora sequor* (Metamorphoses 7:20-12: "I see what is better and approve it, but I follow what is worse").

The "I" that does not understand its own behavior experiences tension, discord and opposition within itself.

"I" realize that sin dwells in my flesh, so that it is no longer I who do it but sin (vv. 16-17). Bad actions seem to assume a super-individual dimension. Fault and responsibility are not denied, but the helplessness of a will which wishes to do good is experienced in a most dramatic way. It is as if the "I" may conclude from the opposition between will and action that this was formerly not so. A demonic power, sin, invaded the "flesh" and established there its dominion (see 5:21). Sin "dwells" (*oikeô*) in me (v. 17b; we find the same verb also in vv. 18a and 20b).

The frequently recurring thematic verb "to want" (*thelô*, vv. 15b, 16a, 18b, 20a and 21a) is further emphasized by *symphêmi* ("to agree," v. 16b) and the still stronger *synêdomai* ("to delight," v. 22). The "I" not only knows what it good but also wants to do it. Wish, consent and delight are, as it were, surrounding the will, but most regrettably the "I" is unable to do what is right.

The Diagnosis (vv. 21-23)

21a So I find it to be a law that when I want to do what is good,
 b evil lies close at hand.
22 For I delight in the law of God in my inmost self,
23 but I see in my members another law at war with the law of my mind, making me captive to the law of sin that dwells in my members.

Verses 21-23 are intended to bring this long exposition to a close. They sound like a conclusive diagnosis. We have already dealt with some expressions and terms: for "my inmost self" (v. 22), "my mind" and "my members" (v. 23) see pp. 50-51; for "to delight" (v. 22) see p. 53.

The fivefold use of "law" (*nomos*) is rather confusing. In verse 21 *nomos* is certainly not the Mosaic law but seems to mean (1) a "rule, principle" which can be recognized as

such through experience. In verses 22-23 there are four more uses:
(2) "the law of God" (= the Mosaic law; see also v. 25b);
(3) "the law of my mind;"
(4) "the law of sin" (see also v. 25b); and
(5) "another law."

The laws of (2) and (3) are positive, those of (4) and (5) negative. The third and fifth expressions point to conflicting tendencies within the human person. The second and fourth expressions refer to realities outside the person, although the fourth reality may have entered the "I" and now dwells within it to keep it captive. Further, it is possible that Paul hardly distinguishes between (4) and (5). We can even ask ourselves whether (1), the "law" of verse 21, is not the result of that "other law" (5) and of "the law of sin" (4), or, even more radically: whether one, four and five do not coincide and correspond in nature, function and character.

No doubt, Paul consciously plays with the concept of *nomos*. He has already done so in 3:21 and 27-28 and will do so again in 8:1-4. In these passages it is not easy for the reader to discern what kind of law or what nuance of it Paul has in view.

"Simul iustus et peccator?" (vv. 24-25)

24a Wretched man that I am!
 b Who will rescue me from this body of death?
25a Thanks be to God through Jesus Christ our Lord!
 b So then, with my mind I am a slave to the law of God, but with my flesh I am a slave to the law of sin.

Exegetes who maintain that by the outcry of verse 24a Paul points to the present Christian condition explain the future tense of the verb in verse 24b eschatologically: "rescue" indicates final salvation. Those, however, who think that Paul, with "wretched man that I am," refers to the unredeemed situation, understand in the deliverance of verse 24b Christ's redeeming death on the cross and its fruit: our justification, already now, in history. That deliverance is no longer future in the real sense, only from the narrative point of view.

Some exegetes of the first category consider verse 25b as the exact equivalent of the famous Lutheran *simul iustus et peccator*. Then the "I" of the regenerate Christian would be at the same time just and sinful. With the mind the "I" serves (*douleuô*, present tense) the law of God, with the flesh simultaneously the law of sin. As will appear later in this book, there are great difficulties involved in this type of interpretation.

The phrase *autos egô* of verse 25b (literally "I myself") is probably not a simple resumption of the "I" in verses 7-23. "I myself" might in this instance have the pregnant sense of "I left to myself," that is without Christ or the Spirit. In this line of thought there may be a shift in the meaning of *douleuô*. We should take it first as a *de conatu* ("I would like to serve the law of God with my mind;" see for example Dieter Zeller, p. 145), and afterwards as the tense of a continuing present reality "with my flesh, however, I am *in fact* serving the law of sin"). If this view regarding the shift in sense is correct, verse 25b then summarizes, after the interruption of verse 24, the entire argument of verses 14-23.

III. Epilogue and questions

It would be worth while to devote more space to the particular Pauline understanding of "sin," "flesh" and "law." Within the framework of this monograph, however, we must limit ourselves. All three notions are no doubt important in Romans 7. Regarding "flesh": in our close reading of the text we have underscored that in Paul the term usually refers to the whole person and, moreover, very often and more specifically in Romans 7:7-25, indicates not simply the person's condition as weak, dependent creature. "Flesh" is the morally weak "I" that is sold into slavery under sin. According to Paul the "law" is the clear expression of God's will and, therefore, holy, just, good and spiritual. However it is Paul's conviction that the "law" has been misused by already present "sin." The "law" becomes an instrument in sin's cunning strategy. By the transgression of the law, "sin" manifests its true nature and increases its sinfulness beyond measure.

There is, however, one specific feature in Romans which above all others intrigues the reader, Paul's use of "I." The problem of the "I" continues to haunt every reader. As a result of our detailed analysis a number of possible interpretations have surfaced: Paul himself, Adam, all human beings, the Jew, the Christian.... We have not yet elaborated on the credentials of these candidates. Of course, not all solutions can be true at the same time. Are they necessarily mutually exclusive? We must thus further investigate the problem of the "I" and try to ground our preference as well as possible. Is the "I" strictly autobiographical? Or has Paul used the "I" metaphorically, in function of a figure or figures in salvation history? If so, does he then refer to Adam, or to the people between Adam and Moses, or to Israel? We have seen that certain elements in the Pauline text strongly suggest a salvation historical approach, but are these elements ultimately decisive?

We shall also have to consider the verbs in verses 7c-11:

what event in the past do they point to? In verses 14b-23 Paul quite unexpectedly uses verbs in the present tense. He seemingly describes an existing tragic situation of the "I." Verse 25a, however, could suggest that this situation no longer exists. Does then, for the redeemed "I" or for the Christian, all that is said in 7:7-25, both the narrative of what happened and the condition resulting from it, lie in the past? Or is the Christian still in a certain but true sense that "wretched" person whom Paul depicts in Romans 7 in such a poignant fashion?

These and similar questions must be dealt with in the next two chapters.

CHAPTER FOUR

Who Is That "I"? Several Proposals

In this chapter we will attempt to present as objectively as possible the most important suggestions which try to identify the "I." In the next chapter a critical choice will be made and our own view and position will be established. How shall we proceed? In a first part we will give the so-called "pure" or basic proposals, in the second the rather composite hypotheses. For each type we begin with an impartial presentation of its elements (a); after that the main difficulties will be brought forward (b). Our exposition will pay special attention to the results of recent publications.

I. Four basic proposals

In Romans 7 it is possible that the "I" has been used by Paul in a literal, autobiographical way. Numerous readers, however, raise the question whether that "I" fulfills a rhetorical function and therefore assumes a figurative sense. If so, there is still more than one possibility.

Paul Himself

a) An easy and seemingly obvious solution holds that Paul is referring to no person other than himself. According to this view, Paul is writing part of his autobiography in 7:7-25. As a boy he did not know the law; he lived outside the law; sin in him was, as it were, dead. Having reached the threshold of manhood, he was subject to the law. He became "son of the law." Latent sin made use of the commandment to seduce and to kill him.

By this text, Paul is providing us with information about the time before his conversion. As a Pharisee he would have fought a hidden but tragic struggle, and, finally, he would have perished through the continuous conflict between his better will and his real activity. The fact of knowing and approving the good, together with the experience of being unable to do it, would have brought him to the verge of ruin and despair. So, in God's plan, the conversion of Paul had been prepared for in a negative way. Knowledge of the law and domination by sin awoke in him the need for deliverance.

Robert H. Gundry is more specific. He is of the opinion that by the commandment, "You shall not covet," (the tenth "word" of the Decalogue) Paul more specifically refers to sexual desire which awakens during puberty. As an unmarried person Paul must have fought against this desire without hope of succes. According to Gundry Paul yielded to the temptation and gravely sinned. That in Philippians 3:4-6 and Galatians 1:13-14 Paul boasts of his religious zeal does not conflict with such a view. Fanatical zeal is outward and visible; Paul's sexual sinfulness was invisible, yet for that matter no less real.

Following Bultmann, Gijs Bouwman and others prefer the "nomistic" interpretation to a general "ethical, antinomistic" one. According to the antinomistic explanation Paul was morally weak, a sinner who transgressed the law. The nomistic interpretation sees Paul's sin in the very observation of the law. In the non-Christian Paul, it is said, there was a religious self-sufficiency. He wanted to use the law of God in function of his own pride. He sinned through legalistic self-aggrandizement and boasting, through works-righteousness. It was a hopeless, disastrous clinging to himself.

b) A first objection against this autobiographical interpretation of the "I" is the unexpected appearance of the first person singular in Romans 7. Otherwise than, for instance, in Phillipians 3, Galatians 1-2 and 2 Corinthians, the context itself does not occasion such a shift to "I" by which, according to this opinion, Paul talks about himself. In Romans 7:4-6 one still finds the inclusive "we" or "us" (Paul and the Roman Christians). Nothing makes it likely that Paul is going to change from the plural to a long passage in the first person singular. A strictly autobiographical "I" would even be more unannounced.

The second objection recalls that Paul in his explicit dealings with his Pharisaic past does not represent it as a despairing existence. On the contrary, he insists on a self-assured life, "as to righteousness under the law, blameless" (Phil 3:6). Gundry's distinction between outward and inward, between visible and hidden, cannot be rejected *a priori*, but is difficult to prove. His sexual interpretation must remain highly hypothetical; it probably will convince only a few.

A third counter-argument is the diatribe style used by Paul here and also elswhere in Romans. Rhetorical questions, personifications and dramatization must be evaluated first of all according to their literary intention. Autobiographical references should not be taken for granted. Does the use of "I" in Romans 7 not belong to this genre?

Finally in regard to sin: in a recent publication on

"desire" in Romans 7:7-8, Heikki Räisänen demonstrates, as others before him have done, that Paul here does not deal with the "nomistic" sin of self-righteousness.

Adam

a) If the "I" of Romans 7:7-25 is not Paul himself, the allusions to the Genesis story may perhaps show that Paul is pointing to Adam, although in contrast with 5:12-21 the name of Adam is not mentioned in this chapter. We must attentively listen to the argumentation of Stanislas Lyonnet.

"Actually ... the data are not missing which prove that he [Paul] was thinking of him [Adam] and of the Genesis narrative where is described first his life of familiarity with God, then his sin and the manner in which the serpent made use of the commandment to arouse the desire of the woman, and, finally, death which our first parents suffered as a punishemnt for their disobedience. In both cases [Genesis 2-3 and Romans 7] we have before us the same persons: (1) a man, type of the human race and in whom this race is, as it were, wholly included so that this man can quite approprately be labeled as an *egô* ("I"); (2) a particular commandment, *entolê*, in the singular in Paul as well as in Genesis; (3) the personified sin, *hê hamartia*, which plays a role analogous to that of the serpent in Genesis and of the devil in the Wisdom passage which had inspired Paul in Romans 5. For in Romans 5:12 he asserted that death came into the world through sin, just as Wisdom 2:24 had said that it came into the world through the envy of the devil" ("L'histoire du salut," p. 133). Lyonnet continues his comparison of the way in which the serpent in Genesis and sin in Romans 7 make use of the prohibition which was meant to bring life, but actually brought death. He concludes that Romans 7, verses 7-12 refer to the Fall of Adam and verses 13-23 describe Adam's condition after the Fall.

Some commentators do take into account the Adam interpretation but they regard the "I" = Adam as a representative of all human beings. In their opinion, the "I" symbolizes every human person. The inner conflict and division can be experienced everywhere and at all times, by everybody. In this view Romans 7 deals with typical and universal human data.

b) The literary impact of Genesis 2-3 upon Roman 5 and 7 can hardly be denied. Yet it seems difficult to admit that the "I" of 7:7-25 should be identified with Adam (or with every human being). Romans 5:12 and 19 mentioned the invasion of sin, and it is precisely these verses which militate against the supposition that sin was already present in Adam before the Fall. This supposition, according to 7:7-12, would be necessary if the "I" of Romans 7 were Adam. The historical pattern in Romans 7 is not:

(A) before the Fall (v. 9a),
(B) from the Fall up to Christ (vv. 9b-24),
(C) from Christ onwards (v. 25a),

but rather, at least for those who defend the following third proposal:

(A) The period between Adam and Moses (before, that is, "apart from the law," v. 9a),
(B) from Moses up to Christ (vv. 9b-24: the Jews under the law),
(C) the period initiated by Christ (v. 25a).

The specific items and allusions in this epistle clearly concern law and Jewish matters and problems. This overall context itself makes it hardly conceivable that Paul was writing in a "timeless" manner and was pointing to universal human experiences and conditions. Moreover, 7:7-23 is framed by passages which proclaim Jesus' deliverance from a sinful state, a past situation, so that the corrrect interpretation cannot but consider the historical sequence of time periods in reference to that major event.

Israel or the Jews under the Law

a) At the end of Romans 7:7 (part of) the tenth commandment of the Decalogue is cited. Does this not indicate that Paul here is thinking of the proclamation of the law on Mount Sinai, especially since Jewish tradition sees "you shall not covet" as the summary of the entire Decalogue? Moreover, verses 8b ("apart from the law sin lies dead") and 9a ("I was once alive apart from the law") remind the reader of Romans 5:12-14 where Paul reflects on the period from Adam to Moses. In this period there was sin, but no real transgression of commandments. For the Decalogue had not yet been proclaimed. It would seem that from all these data the conclusion should be drawn that Romans 7:9b-11, too, refers to the Sinai proclamation, just as the commandment of verse 7e.

Those who defend this third proposal do not deny that Paul depicts sin's deception on the pattern of what the serpent in Genesis did and the devil in Wisdom. Yet the "I," they say, represents Israel. The "I" has, therefore, a collective meaning. In Romans 7:7-11 Paul narrates what sin did with the law after it had been given on Sinai. By misusing the law, sin deceived Israel.

In 7:14-23, after the narrative of verses 8-11, the miserable, hopeless situation of all Jews under the law is described. They are sold as slaves to sin. They boast of their possession of that spiritual law, but since they are "fleshly," they live under the dominion of sin which through the law stirs up in them all kinds of sinful covetousness. Their condition is one of tragic inner conflict and division.

This "salvation historical" interpretation of the "I," recently and forcefully defended by D.J. Moo, would perfectly fit within the broader context of the letter to the Romans. More in particular, without break in the line of thought, 7:7-11 then follows 5:12-14.

b) Yet many hold back from accepting without further ado the identification of Israel with "I." The tragedy which according to its proponents is referred to in Romans 7:8-11 is as such not depicted in the Old Testament. Has Paul been so daringly original that he has transposed motifs from Paradise to the Sinai period?

Christians

The believer is under grace (Rom 6:14). He or she is dead to the law and serves in the new way of the Spirit (7:6). Yet the Christian still lives in the world. Next to these clear "indicative" statements Paul has his numerous "imperative" injunctions and warnings. Galatians 5:16-18 provides us with a good example:

> *16 Live by the Spirit, I say, and do not gratify the desires of the flesh. 17 For what the flesh desires is opposed to the Spirit, and what the Spirit desires is opposed to the flesh; for these are opposed to each other, to prevent you from doing what you want. 18 But if you are led by the Spirit, you are not subject to the law.*

This is almost a parallel text of Romans 7. Galatians 5:17 in particular reminds us of the conflict which Paul works out so broadly in Romans 7.

Many commentators follow Augustine's later explanation (also held by Aquinas) and agree with Luther and his numerous adherents in this matter. They relate Romans 7:7-25 to the struggles which continue to affect every Christian. They call to mind the fact that from 7:14 onwards the verbs are in the present tense. In their opinion 7:25b witnesses to the well-known adage *simul iustus et peccator* (at the same time a righteous person and a sinner). The articles by J.D.G. Dunn and R.Y.K. Fung, as well as the commentaries by John Murray, C.K. Barrett, C.E.B Cranfield and Dunn continue to defend this fourth view vigorously. They argue that after justification and baptism the painful tension between Spirit and flesh survives. In their view the positive statement regarding the "I," as well as the inmost self and the mind, point to the regenerate condition. Just as the pious ancestors of the Old Testament and the saints of all times, so also the converted Paul remained conscious of his sinfulness and helpless misery. Even after baptism, sin and grace struggle with each other within the same person. What is depicted in Romans 8, in the life of a Christian, does not come after Romans 7; the two situations exist simultaneously, in one and the same Christian. The tension between Romans 7 and Romans 8, a tension between "not yet" and "already," is typical of Christian existence until the close of the ages.

Sometimes this interpretation is somewhat mitigated through the qualification that the struggle is particularly heavy at the beginning of the regenerate life of the Christian (see for example the commentary of A.F.N. Lekkerkerker, p. 315: the believer who *begins* to be justified in the midst of sin) or through the admission that a conflict such as described in Romans 7 is not the normal situation of the Christian (so Fung).

b) No doubt in Galatians 5:16-18 Paul addresses his fellow Christians, and his warnings are meant for their persistent struggle. In this passage the Spirit who brings effective assistance is very much brought into prominence. In Romans 7, however, there is no mention at all of God's Spirit. That is the big difference between the two passages. To be sure, by means of the expression the "inmost self" (*esô anthrôpos*, 7:22) and the term the "mind" (*nous*, 7:23 and 25) something positive is said about the "I," but these "natural" factors in all probability do not suppose the presence of the Spirit. The "I" is still unredeemed, not yet regenerate.

It must be added that one does not see where, in this fourth proposal, the tragic event of 7:7-11 could be placed in the life of the Christian. Further, the reference to the saints with their sharp consciousness of sin, in itself a valid point, is in this context not completely cogent.

II. Composite Proposals

Various interpretations of the "I" in Romans 7 which combine elements from more than one proposal have been worked out.

Fusion

Cranfield, for example, maintains that in verses 7-13 Paul refers to himself as the representative of all human beings, while in verses 14-25 he speaks of Christians in general (*Romans*, p. 345). We find more or less the same position in Dunn who explicitly mentions Paul's pre-Christian experience (*Romans*, p. 382). Moo claims that Paul, above all, deals with Israel but also, to a certain extent, is speaking of himself (p. 123): Romans is simultaneously an "objective narrative" and a "subjective confession" (p. 129). In his publications, John A. Ziesler defends the position that, for Paul, Adam is the model, but that Paul uses Adam to allude to himself as a type of all human beings. Finally, Lekkerkerker concludes: "The *Urgeschichte* [the history of the origin] which is described in verses 7-12 is the heading above the life of all of us. It is the history of Adam *and* Israel *and* the church *and* Paul himself" (*Aan de Romeinen*, p. 304).

The Psychological "I"

We would like to pay more attention to the so-called psychological interpretation. This approach, too, combines elements from different views, but its focus is on the subconscious regions in the human being. This makes it an interpretation in its own right.

In 1971, the well-known Leuven psychologist, Antoon Vergote, devoted a study to Romans 7 which was well received by a number of exegetes. Paul-Emile Langevin, for instance, not only reviewed the main results of that study, but also discussed its methodological implications. In *Psychologische Aspekte paulinischer Theologie* (1983), Gerd Theissen wrote more than a hundred dense pages about Romans 7. In recent publications quite often reference is made to this thorough study. We first attempt to gather the more important data and, then, we venture an evalution.

a) Just as in some of the other aforementioned proposals, in this new approach, too, the Paradise narrative of Genesis is the starting point. But for the psychological interpretation, what is said about Adam applies to every human being.

What Paul elaborates in Romans 7:7-25 would still witness to a conflict which has been present in his subconscious life. That conflict must be compared with the Oedipus complex: the exaggerated feeling of a son toward his mother (or of the daughter toward her father) with, at the same time, jealousy of the parent of the same sex. When unresolved in the child, that unbalanced love may develop into a source of personality disorder. This tension, of course, exists in the subconscious zones of human life.

The three (mainly subconscious) phases in the human evolution toward adulthood are compared with the phases of the "I" in Romans 7.

(1) First there is life without law, an indefinite situation, an vague, undefinable innocence, a seemingly boundless desire and a strong bond with the mother. Compare Romans 7:8b-9a: "Apart from the law sin lies dead; I was once alive apart from the law."

(2) Then begins the inner conflict, the revolt against the father, the confrontation with prescriptions and prohibitions, that is, against the law which comes from the outside. Compare Romans 7:7de-8a: "Yet, if it had not been for the law, I would not have known sin. I would not have known what it is to covet if the law had not said, 'You shall not covet.' But sin, seizing an opportunity, through the commandment produced in me all kinds of covetousness" (see also v. 11). Paul elaborates this conflict in verses 14-25. Freud's famous trio may be present in Romans 7: the *Id* (= the "flesh"); the *Ego* (= the "I"); and the *Superego* (= the "law").

(3) In the third phase the reconciliation with the father takes place, a kind of identification of father and son. The tension is resolved. The desires are transformed and raised to a higher level. A real awakening, a becoming aware occurs in this phase; it is accompanied by personal, more

and more "adult" decisions. Compare what Paul writes in 7:24b and chapter 8 about deliverance and new life.

The first two phases develop in the subconscious regions of the personality. Only in the third phase does one reach full self-consciousness and become able to decide one's own destiny in a responsible fashion. Sometimes psychological maturity is not easily attained; a disorder may appear. One of the therapies consists in the awakening of the second phase, that of the conflict. Without the help of a therapist, the patient is often unable to do this.

We can hardly avoid the question: is Romans 7 not such a document of developing awareness?

Within this context, Theissen discusses Philippians 3, especially verses 5 and 6: "... as to zeal, a persecutor of the church; as to righteousness under the law, blameless. Yet whatever gains I had, these I have come to regard as loss because of Christ." According to Theissen we see before us the proud, aggressive Paul, the Pharisee who ardently works for the law and merciless persecuted "heretics." That demonstrative self-righteousness is, in Theissen's opinion, the result of Paul's reaction against the law conflict which is present in his subconscious life (and which, in Romans 7, breaks through into full awareness).

In Romans 2:17-23 Paul is, at it were, himself the therapist for others, his fellow Jews. He attempts to pierce the feeling of superiority which the sinful Jews publicly demonstrate, and lays open their real inner condition:

> *17 But if you call yourself a Jew and rely on the law and boast of your relation to God 18 and know his will and determine what is best because you are instructed in the law, 19 and if you are sure that you are a guide to the blind, a light to those who are in darkness, 20 a corrector of the foolish, a teacher of children, having in the law the embodiment of knowledge and*

> *truth, 21 you, then, that teach others, will you not teach yourself? While you preach against stealing, do you steal? 22 You that forbid adultery, do you commit adultery? You that abhor idols, do you rob temples? 23 You that boast in the law, do you dishonor God by breaking the law?*

What Paul does for his fellow Jews in Romans 2, that he does, according to Theissen, for himself and all Jews (and human beings) in Romans 7.

b) We cannot but concede that the similarity of the threefold structure is striking. Yet, without denying, or even underestimating, that whole complex and mysterious world of the subconscious, without casting doubt upon the merits of psychoanalysis and its healing efforts, we must point out the major differences between what Paul says and what a psychological or psychoanalytical approach teaches.

Presumably Paul fully realized the hopeless situation of the unredeemed only trough his new life in Christ. Yet, we must ask the question whether Romans 7 can really be called a document of a healing awareness. Moreover, the three phases in becoming an adult are a natural process. Everybody must experience that development; sometimes a therapist can be of help. Paul, however, speaks of human sin and divine liberation. He concludes Romans 7 with, "thanks be to God through Jesus Christ our Lord!" (v. 25a). Finally, the correctness of Theissen's interpretation of Philippians 3 is questionable indeed. Paul's alleged pride and agressiveness, his zeal for the law and his persecution of Christians can hardly be explained as a result of the subconscious conflict of the law within himself. We will have to return to this passage.

III. Brief Conclusion

This long overview undoubtedly possesses many interesting features which the search for the identity of Paul's "I" in Romans 7 cannot neglect. Yet no proposal of our fourth chapter is totally convincing. In each case, objections have been brought forward. Is the "I" radically fictitious or is it perhaps thorougly autobiographical? Or is it to a certain extent both at the same time? Is what Paul describes regarding the inner division totally unrelated to the justified, already liberated life of the Christian? Or, on the contrary, are Christians, as long as they live on earth, themselves those "wretched" creatures? To what degree is the human person conditioned in his or her sinfulness by heredity and environment?

We repeat the initial question: can we solve all these problems? How precisely must we nuance what Paul means by his use of "I"?

CHAPTER FIVE

The Identity of the "I"

At the beginning his 1932 study on Romans 7 Rudolf Bultmann writes: "It seems to me that these questions [respecting the identity of the "I"] have sufficiently been discussed and that the answer cannot be doubted. The situation characterized here is that of the man who is under law, and more precisely, his situation as it became manifest to the eyes of one who, through Christ, has been set free from the law" (p. 198). Bultmann thus corroborates the position of the pioneering investigation of Werner G. Kümmel in 1929. Today we can no longer speak of a generally accepted consensus.

After the examination of the main proposals in the preceding chapter, three questions remain without clear answer. Firstly, whom does Paul intend by the "I" of Romans 7? Secondly, which event is referred to in verse 9b by "but when the commandment came, sin sprang to life," and in what period of time did (or does) the situation depicted in verses 14-23 exist? Thirdly, what kind of sin does Paul speak of, and how is this sin related to the law? The critical survey of chapter four already suggests that not every answer to these questions will be black-and-white. One will have to take into account various and differing data.

A threefold approach may help us in determining the identity of the "I." We shall successively pay attention to the literary character of the pericope, the salvation historical references within the passage, and the existential quality of Paul's discourse.

I. DOES PAUL MEAN HIMSELF?

Personifications of law and sin, as well as the sudden appearance of the "I," are characteristic of Romans 7. These "persons" meet each other and influence each other. The "I" is passive and powerless. Romans 7 is a highly dramatized representation. One must assess its literary features carefully. In the first part of this chapter attention is given to the evaluation of the literary character of the pericope. In order better to determine the autobiographical density, we compare Romans 7 with 1 Corinthians 6:12-20 and Galatians 2:18-21, two passages where the "I" also occurs. Moreover, the Galatian text will be helpful in our closer look at the inner conflict of the "I" in Romans 7.

A Rhetorical "I"

With regard to Romans 7 one could accuse Paul of exaggeration, for example where he says or suggests that all the "I" does is (always) sin. One could also remark that such assertions do not concur with what he says elsewhere in the letter. In 2:14, for example, Paul seems to accept the possibility that (at least some) Gentiles who do not have the law do what the law requires. How can this be in agreement with the total absence of good action in the "I"?

Willem Grossouw rightly notes that Paul as a good dramatist had to heighten and to simplify. Paul "works out a kind of abstraction, not one, however, which depicts from the concrete reality, but one which intensifies the experience of reality by concentrating it into its essential dimensions. By this operation a picture of life arises which is intensified as well as simplified but rests on the basis of the most authentic reality." Paul had to depict as sharply as possible the contrast between light and darkness: "real existential experience is set in bright light. A specific vision allows directions and possibilities to be carried forward and presented as absolute while others disappear or fall into the background. In Romans 7 this vision is the Christian faith vision concerning the existence without Christ which has been reflected upon in a radical way" (pp. 78-79).

Romans 7 therefore discloses a "concentrated authenticity of life." This certainly means that we should not underestimate the rhetorical character of the "I." But is all said by this? Does the rhetorical outlook unavoidably exclude autobiography? If anything, does "concentrated authenticity of life" not point precisely to Paul himself?

To a Great Extent Autobiographical

Paul's use of the "I" in his letters is sometimes impersonal or supra-individual. In the discussion on sexual laxity, he writes in the first letter to the Corinthians: "'All things are lawful for me,' but I will not be dominated by anything" (6:12). And further, in 6:15b: "Should I ... take the members of Christ and make them members of a prostitute? Never!" It is quite possible that in verse 12 Paul cites a slogan of his opponents. In verse 15b, moreover, we have before us the diatribe style already familiar to us (see pp. 31-33). In this passage of 1 Corinthians, it is obvious that Paul does not mean himself, certainly not primarily. What he says about the "I" applies to every Christian. The "I" of 1 Corinthians 6:12 is decidedly rhetorical and supra-individual.

In the analysis of Romans 7 reference is often made to Galatians 2:18-21. In verses 15-17 Paul has used the first person plural. After the incident of Antioch (2:11-14), Paul's use of "we" points to Peter and himself: "we ourselves are Jews by birth" (v. 15). In verse 18 he suddenly shifts to the first person singular: "But if I build up again the very things that I once tore down, then I demonstrate that I am a transgressor." What he expresses here is in fact applicable to Peter and only in a hypothetical manner to himself. The use of "I" in verse 18 is therefore rhetorical, in the sense that Paul indirectly, but really, rebukes Peter by it.

That is, I think, no longer the case in what follows. To be sure, the content of verses 19-21 applies to every Christian. Yet, it would seem that Paul here, above all, speaks of his personal inner conviction and deepest experience:

> *19 For through the law I died to the law, so that I might live to God. I have been crucified with Christ; 20 and it is no longer I who live, but it is Christ who lives in me. And the life I now live in the flesh I live by faith in the Son of God, who loved me and gave himself for me. 21 I do not nullify the grace of God; for if justification comes through the law, then Christ died for nothing.*

This "I" in Galatians 2:19-21 is most probably autobiographical, at least in the first instance.

Besides the possible rhetorical use of "I," there is in Paul's letters yet another objection against the autobiographical interpretation, namely the content itself. The innerly divided Paul of Romans 7 stands over and against the zealous, self-assured Paul of Philippians 3! Nobody doubts the sincerity of Paul's witness in the last passage. Before his conversion, he was perfect, blameless "as to righteousness under the law" (Phil 3:6; see also Gal 1:14: "I advanced in Judaism beyond many among my people of the same age, for I was far more zealous for the traditions of my ancestors"). Romans 7 and Philippians 3, it is said, cannot be both autobiographical at the same time.

In the last chapter we mentioned Gundry's distinction between innerly sexually sinful (Romans 7) and outwardly fanatically blameless (Philippians 3). One rightly hesitates to assume the narrow sexual interpretation of the commandment, "you shall not covet" (Romans 7:7e). Yet Gundry's study may provide us with a useful distinction between inner (invisible) and outer (visible).

As is well known, Paul in Romans 7:7e (and 13:9) omits all the directs objects after "you shall not covet": house, the neighbor, his wife, male or female slave, ox or donkey. This omission has often been explained as an intended generalization. Desire is the root and source of all sins. By means of one (shortened) commandment the whole law would have been meant. Ziesler, however, strongly opposes this assumption. In his opinion, Paul very much focuses on the tenth commandment alone. By the specific term "to covet" only this commandment fits well the description of Romans 7:14-25; the other "words" of the Decalogue do not. For the great majority of people "outwardly" observe most commandments. They can honestly say that they do not wrongly use the name of the Lord, that they honor their father and mother, that they do not murder nor commit adultery, that they do not steal .... But what about the inner desires and secret cravings: who among us can claim to be without a multitude of hidden sins? Moreover, it is precisely this last and tenth commandment which incites to other (outward) sins.

One can therefore, it would seem, hold that Romans 7

and Philippians 3 are autobiographically reconcilable. According to this view, in Romans 7 Paul would concede that, notwithstanding his outward radical religious stand and zeal for the law, his inner desires were not without sinful covetousness.

There is also the style itself. In the final analysis, even the highly passionate, personal style with the "I" appears to plead for a strong autobiographical dimension of the passage. Although one must certainly reckon with the literary and thus conventional, artificial character of the "I" in Romans 7, it cannot be denied that in this pericope Paul speaks in a vivid, emotional and pathetic manner. Personal experience is presumably to a large extent responsible for this kind of speech.

Should we assume that this experience comes from both his pre-Christian life (as seen now after conversion) and his Christian existence, albeit it in a differing way? This question must be answered, I think, in the affirmative. Paul is writing about things he too has felt and undergone, notwithstanding his (past) Pharisaic fanaticism and (present) Christian ardor. There must have been conflict and tension also in him. Grossouw states it rather carefully. "Paul would not have been able to picture in Romans 7 the human situation in such an authentic and dramatic way, if he had not experienced it as his own possibility, and this not only as an (eventually) actualized possibility of his Jewish past but also as a yet real possibility which could pervert also his Christian existence" (p. 80). Grossouw, however, does not so much see Paul's sin as moral weakness, but more as spiritual self-sufficiency. Is this correct?

Transgression of the Law

One gets the impression that, in Galatians 2:18 and 21, Paul fears that building up again what has been demolished (the law) will imply nullifying God's grace and work in Christ. For Paul, remaining subject to the law would then become sinful beyond measure. Also in Romans 9:32 and 10:2-3 Paul discusses the tragic situation of the Jews: notwithstanding their zeal for God, they are not enlightened; they do not understand the way God now justifies; they stumble over Jesus Christ, the stumbling block; they seek to establish their own righteousness and are unwilling to submit to that of God.

Does Paul in Romans 7 have in mind this Jewish blindness? Does the failure of the "I" consist in striving for its own righteousness and a rejection of Christ? Or, in a still more radical sense: does the failure, as Bultmann claims, transcend the individual in such a way that existence itself is perverted? Is, therefore, human effort to keep the law affected in its root by sinful egotism and pride? Does sin manifest itself even in the observance of the law? Is sin therefore above all "nomistic"?

It seems to me that in chapter seven of Romans nothing points to such an interpretation. Paul concretely has in mind the transgression of the commandment, the non-observance of the law. Herman Ridderbos, for instance, rightly underscores this in his well-known book on Paul (see pp. 153-160). The sinfulness dealt with in Romans 7 is "anti-nomistic." The "I" has been betrayed and seduced; the "I" is carnal, sold into slavery under sin. The "I" does not do what is prescribed by the law, although the "I" delights — which is certainly positive — in God's law. With the mind the "I" wants to be a slave of the law of God —

and this desire is certainly a good thing — but in fact the "I" sins with the "flesh" by transgressing the law.

II. ALLUSIONS TO SALVATION HISTORY

Commentators have tried to see the "I" as representing every human being. Romans 7 would give a description of a general human situation, the tragic condition of people of all times and places. Text and context, however, do not seem to allow such a broad interpretation. With the "I" Paul must have had in mind a person who belongs to the Jewish people. After all, Romans 7 does contain a defense of the law, the Torah. The commandment was intended "for life" (v. 10b). Although the law has been misused, the law remains holy, and the commandment holy, just and good (v. 12). The law is spiritual (v. 14a). In verse 7e a commandment from this law is explicitly cited, the tenth "word" of the Decalogue. No doubt, the tragic event alluded to by Paul in verses 7-13 is not without a salvation historical dimension.

A question remains as to precisely what event Paul refers in verses 9-10a: "I was once alive apart from the law, but when the commandment came, sin revived and I died." Three views have been proposed.

Paul's Own Growth?

In 1 Corinthians 12:31 Paul addresses the Christians: "Strive for the greater gifts. And I will show you a still more excellent way." After this truly authorial "I," Paul shifts to the rhetorical "I" which, however, must not completely exclude a reference to Paul himself: "If I speak in the tongues of mortals and angels, but do not have love, I am a noisy gong ...." In verse 11 of this lyric chapter, we read: "When I was a child, I spoke like a child, I thought like a child, I reasoned like a child; when I became an adult, I put an end to childish ways." Still a rhetorical "I." Yet Paul speaks of infancy.

So we are brought to the question whether in Romans 7, too, Paul does not speak of years long gone, of his own youth. In the Middle Ages, and still today, a ceremony exists through which the Jewish boy of the age of thirteen becomes *barmitzvah*, "Son of the Commandment." From that age onwards the Jew must keep the whole law. The idea must have existed long before the ceremony. At the onset of puberty, when adulthood is going to be reached, Jews are fully confronted with the law.

At first sight, Romans 7:7-13 seems to fit this state of affairs perfectly. The explanation runs as follows. Paul speaks of his youth. He had not yet known sin; he had not yet experienced sinful desires. To be sure, because of Adam's Fall sin was present, also in Paul, but apart from the law sin was, at it were, dead. Once, without the law, Paul was alive. When puberty arrived, Paul experienced for the first time what the law meant by "you shall not covet." Sin springs to life; sin seizes the opportunity and, through the commandment, betrays Paul and leads him to death. Now, after conversion, Paul is clearly aware of this tragic event. He can accurately depict its consequences in verses 14-23. Paul confesses: my condition as an adult, pre-Christian Jew was completely hopeless and incurable; Christ alone can rescue me from this existence of death.

According to this tempting interpretation, the "I" is totally autobiographical. Yet, not all details of the text find their place in it. So, reading verse 7, one does not immediately think of a developing subjective awareness during the process of maturation; rather, one thinks of a proclamation of the law which comes from the outside. Furthermore, in this interpretation does verse 9, if it deals with life without law, speak of "real" life? And can one maintain that during their early years Jewish children are completely outside the law, that they live apart from the law? Moreover, the pericope contains unequivocal allusions to Adam and unredeemed Israel.

Altogether these objections together make it rather doubtful that in verses 7-13 Paul was thinking of his infancy years and the transition to adulthood.

The Fall of Adam

In the narrative of the Fall in Genesis 3, the woman answers God's question, "What is this you have done?" with "The serpent tricked me...." In Romans 7:11 Paul writes: "Sin, seizing an opportunity, through the commandment deceived me ...." As we have seen, in the Greek version of Genesis the verb for "to trick" is almost the same as that for "to deceive" in Romans 7 (see p. 47). Such an agreement is hardly accidental. While composing Romans 7:11 Paul must have had the story of the Fall in mind.

There are more data in Romans 7:7-13 which point to Genesis (see pp. 62-63 in our fourth chapter). The most important are: a life apart from the law and then the arrival of the commandment, the misuse of the commandment by sin with death as a result, and the strong emphasis on life and death in the whole passage.

Those who hesitate to assume that with the "I" Paul was thinking of Adam point out that in this pericope Adam is not even mentioned by name, that in Genesis 3:13 not Adam but the woman is seduced by the serpent, and that in Romans 7,7e the Decalogue, not the prohibition from Genesis 3, is cited; further, that in Genesis 3, contrary to Romans 7:8-9, sin did not exist before the Fall, and that already in Romans 5:12-14 Paul had dealt with the entrance of sin in the world and with Adam's Fall.

It must be said that most of these difficulties do not carry much weight. In order to refer to a person one must not always name that person. There is hardly any difference between Adam and the woman as far as the Fall is concerned. True, according to Genesis 2-3 sin was not present in Paradise before the Fall, but — it could be argued — the serpent was there anyway. Furthermore, in Israel traditional belief connected the Genesis commandment with the Sinai law: both prohibit the desire of what is not permitted. The very fact that already in Romans 5:12-14 Adam is explicitly spoken of makes it easier to accept allusion to him in 7:7-13 as well.

What conclusion can be drawn from these somewhat contradictory arguments? One should perhaps assume that in Romans 7 Paul re-read Genesis 3 with new eyes (so, for instance, Rudolf Pesch in his commentary). There can be no doubt that Paul has used motifs from Genesis. Even more: Paul sees what the serpent did to Adam by means of the commandment as the type of what (personified) sin did to the Jews and himself by means of the law. Reading Romans 7:7-13 one cannot but spontaneously think of Adam's Fall. Yet Adam is only the model. Through the example of Adam Paul wants to see Israel and, more specifically, the Israelite he himself was. The conflict situation depicted in Romans 7:14-23, is not that of Adam, but that of the Jew under the law, more in particular, his own condition before the redemption brought by Christ.

Unredeemed Israel

There are three reasons for assuming that Paul in Romans 7 was thinking of Israel as a whole and not only of himself.

(1) In Romans 7:7 the tenth commandment of the Decalogue is quoted. Moreover, through the distinction in verses 8-9 between "once" (that is the period before the law), and "'when' the commandment came," the readers are, it could be said, reminded of the giving of the law on Mount Sinai.

(2) That recalling to mind in Romans 7 is supported by what Paul wrote in 5:12-14. In 5:13-14 he deals with the period between Adam and Moses. Sin, which entered into the world through one man, remains there; but in this period sin is not "reckoned" since the law is not yet proclaimed. "Apart from the law sin lies dead" (7:8). When the commandment comes, that is, when Israel receives the law at Sinai, then sin springs to life, or better, *re*vives (*anazaô*, see p. 48), after sin has lived a first time in Adam (7:9). Sin seizes, as it were, the law and, through the law, betrays and kills Israel (7:10-11). The tragic consequences are depicted in 7:14-25. Although Israel possesses the holy and spiritual law, this same Israel is sold into slavery under sin. Until the coming of Christ we have, therefore, an Israel under the law, an unredeemed Israel.

(3) One should not be amazed that Paul rhetorically identifies himself with Israel. The prophets had done likewise. See Jeremiah 10:19-20:

> *19 Woe is me because of my hurt! My wound is severe. But I said, "Truly this is my punishment, and I must bear it." 20 My*

> *tent is destroyed, and all my cords are broken; my children have gone from me, and they are no more, there is no one to spread my tent again, and to set up my curtains.*

Reference could also be made to Micah 7:7-10 and Lamentations 1:9-22. In such passages as these the "I" represents the collective Israel. Why could Paul, then, not identify himself with his people?

Must we draw the conclusion from all this that Paul, in Romans 7, had explicitly in mind Israel's confrontation with the law at Sinai? A positive answer to this question would, I think, go too far. Neither the Old Testament nor Jewish tradition speak of sin which itself, as it were tactically and intentionally, misuses the proclaimed law. Yet, this way of reasoning which Paul links with the Sinai proclamation elsewhere in Romans is not altogether absent from Romans 7. For "apart from the law sin lies dead" (7:8) recalls 5:20 ("law came in, with the result that the trespass multiplied") and 4:15 ("where there is no law, neither is there violation"). Further, verses 14 and 21 of Romans 5 deal with the domination of sin through death. This motif, too, is present in Romans 7.

Would the "I" of Romans 7 be, therefore, nothing more than a symbol for the pre-Christian, unredeemed Israel, for all Jews without Christ? No. Most probably Paul meant by the "I" first of all himself. After his conversion he must have realized clearly that he himself has been that Jew under the law, a Jew without Christ.

III. Existential Character

The term "existential" is here to be taken in a double sense. We must assume that Romans 7 cannot haven been written by Paul without his existential experience as Christian, without his retrospective view of his Jewish past. This is the first meaning of the term. The second meaning concerns the Christian status of the present readers of Romans 7: is this text still relevant and, if so, what is its existential significance for their life today?

A Retrospective of the Unregenerate Past

It is not superfluous to stress once more that Romans 7 was written by Paul *after* his conversion. Only through justification has he achieved the correct insight into the actual tragic condition of his pre-Christian existence as Jew. One can estimate sin in all its negative dimensions only after having been set free from its domination. Romans 7 especially describes the not yet converted Paul, Paul under the law, in his hopeless situation confronted with this law. The dark, negative side of such a life was not fully realized by Paul prior to the Damascus event. Paul composed Romans 7 with a Christian view of this pre-Christian existence. Antoon Vergote formulates this beautifully: "Il s'agit d'une relecture du passé, avec la grille de la foi" (p. 121; in a free paraphrase: Paul re-reads the past through the prism of faith). Vergote refers to Augustine who re-read his past and published this retrospective as *confessiones* in the twofold sense of the word: confession of sin and confession of faith.

The picture which Paul draws of himself (and the Jew) before and without Christ is not totally negative. To be sure, the hopeless inner division of the "I," its conflict and powerlessness, are very much highlighted. Yet, within the "I," besides the will to do the good, there is also the consciousness of this wretched condition, together with the knowledge that God's commandment is good and even together with the delight in the law. Thus we are somewhat reminded of passages where Paul deals with the universal, factual knowledge of God (see 1:19-21) and with the eventual moral integrity of the Gentiles (see 2:14-16: some of them instinctively do what the law requires), however different these ideas remain from those in Romans 7.

One can ask why Paul in this section of his letter, devoted to the justified life of the Christian (chapters 5-8), speaks at such length of this pre-Christian, unregenerate situation, a condition of death. Our answer must refer to what has already been underlined: only through and after justification Paul did duly realize his pre-Christian state of estrangement and misery. This is, however, not yet the entire answer. Is Paul's very intention in Romans 7, is his ultimate purpose not to stimulate full knowledge, not of death, but of new life in Christ? Through the negative picture of the Jew before and without Christ he evidently wants to promote the appreciation of Christian existence and, at the same time, to encourage a life which corresponds to the gift of the Spirit. The past, being remembered, is *per se* not really past but present. Only after deliverance do we understand what it was to be captive. Nonetheless, at the same time, it is only against that negative background that we are able to appreciate fully what it means to be free.

Relevance for the Christian Future

The more one admits that contemporary exegesis has advanced valid, conclusive arguments which enable us to safely say that the "I" of Romans 7 is not to be identified with the regenerate believer, the Christian under grace, the more the question remains why so many Christians formerly and nowadays find in Romans 7 a telling description of dimensions of their own Christian existence. At the beginning of his monograph, Kümmel formulates the problem as follows: "How is it to be explained that our Christianity differs so widely from the Pauline one that we actually recognize ourselves in the picture of the Pauline non-Christian?" (*Römer 7*, p. 1). Three considerations may assist us to approach a solution of this problem.

(1) It is typical of Paul who emphasizes at any occasion God's salvific initiative that he stresses again and again the necessity of the human response. As long as the Christian is in the flesh, he or she must be exhorted not to live according to the "flesh." In the last chapter we have noticed that, apart from the presence or absence of the Spirit, there is almost no difference in expression between Romans 7 and Galatians 5. See, for instance, Galatians 5:17: "What the flesh desires is opposed to the Spirit, and what the Spirit desires is opposed to the flesh; for these are opposed to each other ...." The conflict and radical powerlessness within the non-Christian comes back, as it were, in a kind of inner division which Christians experience in the midst of their struggle on earth to live a truly Christian life.

(2) The great majority of North-Atlantic Christians have not tasted that overwhelming joy to which Romans 7:24-25a witnesses: "Wretched man that I am! Who will rescue me from this body of death? Thanks be to God through Jesus our Lord!" In his commentary Dieter Zeller notes that a Western Christian has been baptized as a new-born baby and has mostly been raised in a Christian family, in a society which still preserves Christian values. For such a Christian the unfamiliarity with a real conversion may result in a less characteristic, often weakened Christian life. Does this not lead to a blurring and a fading of the

boundaries between Christian and non-Christian so that the situation of Romans 7 is not completely absent from such a (Christian) life?

(3) The significance of Romans 7 for our Christian existence lies above all in its implicit warning intensity. A Christian may be in danger of falling back into a pre-Christian mentality. Christians can begin with the Spirit and end with the flesh. In Romans 8 Paul writes: "Those who live according to the flesh set their minds on the things of the flesh .... The mind that is set on the flesh is hostile to God; it does not submit to God's law — indeed it cannot, and those who are in the flesh cannot please God .... If you live according to the flesh, you will die" (vv. 5a, 7-8 and 13a). Through moral weakness and a multitude of sins each of us can become a slave of sin and then experience the situation of inner conflict and misery which Paul has described in 7:14-23.

In his final considerations Zeller also rightly remarks that in Romans 7 Paul has spoken, of course, out of his own cultural surroundings and circumstances. Therefore, in his description Paul could not take into account the findings of modern science about the subconscious and heredity. Neither was Paul equipped with our present feeling for the structural and social dimensions of sin. An actualization of Romans 7 will certainly have to incorporate these and similar important insights.

IV. Conclusion

At the end of this lengthy search for the identity of the "I" in Romans 7, the result remains still somewhat uncertain. It appears to me that one must not defend a single proposal to the exclusion of the others. During the course of our discussion many nuances have been introduced. What is our conclusion?

It would seem that the "I" is more autobiographical than is accepted in most contemporary publications. The picture of Paul's pre-Christian situation appears to be more Jewish than many interpretations which accentuate a universal human application suggest. The certainly rhetorical quality of the "I" should not disguise the pre-eminently personal character of this Pauline chapter. Once sufficient attention is given to the inner dimensions of the cited commandment in Romans 7:7e ("you shall not covet"), the autobiographical understanding does not contradict, I think, Paul's utterances elsewhere about his blameless Jewish past.

In Romans 7 Paul has depicted his pre-Christian, not his Christian, situation. We, present-day Christians, cannot agree with the Lutheran *simul iustus et peccator* (at the same time righteous and sinner). The adage, at least in the way most commentators understand it, is incorrect and, moreover, dangerous. The indwelling Spirit will never admit a compromise between righteousness and sin. Christians should not resign themselves to evil as if it were unavoidable.

All Christians, however, have experiences in their lives which are similar to those of Paul's Jewish past. So they fear for themselves. Paul's past could become one's present. Even hope which is grounded in the Spirit must not take away this healthy fear. Christians should beware of a pseudo-confidence, a false peace. Christians must thank God for the freedom brought by Jesus: there is no condemnation for those who are in Christ Jesus (Romans 8:1). However, against the dark background of Romans 7, they very much realize that the "just requirement" of the law of the Spirit must be fulfilled through a life "according to the Spirit" (8:4).

It may be true that in Romans 7 Paul is depicting himself as a wretched man in order to warn his fellow Christians not to fall back into the former unregenerate state. It may also be true that Paul does not stop recommending a life according to the Spirit. Above all, however, we should keep in mind that for Paul the possibility of such a life is given by God, earned by Jesus Christ his Son, and activated in the Christian by the indwelling Spirit.

CHAPTER SIX

Christian Certainty of Salvation (Romans 8:1-17 and 31-39)

In Romans 7:24-25a Paul writes: "Wretched man that I am! Who will rescue me from this body of death? Thanks be to God through Jesus Christ our Lord!" After this complaining question and utterance of thanks, Paul once more summarizes the pre-Christian situation: "So then, I, left to myself, with my mind I try to be a slave to the law of God, but with my flesh I am a slave to the law of sin." Chapter 8 is connected with the thanksgiving of 7:25a which had already announced the great shift: "There is ... now no condemnation for those who are in Christ Jesus" (8:1). The entire chapter 8 is characterized by a striking certainty of faith. So we read in verse 11 that God who raised Christ Jesus from the dead will also give life to the mortal body of the Christian through the power of the Spirit, and in verse 17 that Christians together with Christ will be heirs of God and will participate in the glorification of Christ. In verse 18 Paul says: "I consider that the sufferings of this present time are not worth comparing with the glory about to be revealed to us," and in verse 30 he even uses a past tense: God *has* glorified those whom he has justified. In verse 28 one reads: "We know that all things work together for good for those who love God," and, again, in verses 38-39: "I am convinced" that nothing "will be able to separate us from the love of God in Christ Jesus our Lord."

Chapter 8 can be divided into three units: verses 1-17, 18-30 and 31-39. In the first unit Paul explains what a life according to the Spirit looks like, what it leads to and what it should bring forth. In the second unit he discusses the eager longing for freedom from bondage which is present both in creation and in the Christian. The broad, solemn style of the third unit identifies it clearly as a conclusion: if God is for us, no one can be against us and nothing can separate us from the love of God in Christ Jesus.

Since Paul in verse 18 opposes the present "light" sufferings to the "heavier" future glory (for the contrast "light-heavy," see 2 Cor 4:17), the reader expects the development of this particular theme. What is worked out in verses 19-27, however, is the longing for glory. Verses 20-22 more specifically deal with the "groaning creation" and its craving for wholeness. Because of the importance and actuality of this subject, we will devote the entire next chapter to the examination of Romans 8:18-30. Therefore, in this sixth chapter that middle section is omitted. Moreover, no detailed exegesis of the first and third unit will be provided. We proceed to a close reading of Romans 8:1-17 and 31-39 and analyze the train of thought in these pericopes. We also reflect on "the life according to the Spirit" and on Paul's remarkable certainty of salvation.

I. Led by the Spirit (Romans 8:1-17)

After a first reading of the text we will analyze Paul's reasoning. We will conclude with a consideration of the Spirit who dwells in the Christian.

The Text

1 There is therefore now no condemnation for those who are in Christ Jesus.
2 For the law of the Spirit of life in Christ Jesus has set you free from the law of sin and of death.
3a For God has done what the law, weakened by the flesh, could not do:
 b by sending his own Son in the likeness of sinful flesh, and as a sin offering, he condemned sin in the flesh,
4 so that the just requirement of the law might be fulfilled in us, who walk not according to the flesh but according to the Spirit.
5a For those who live according to the flesh set their minds on the things of the flesh,
 b but those who live according to the Spirit set their minds on the things of the Spirit.
6a To set the mind on the flesh is death,
   but to set the mind on the Spirit is life and peace.
7a For this reason the mind that is set on the flesh is hostile to God;
 b it does not submit to God's law —
 c indeed it cannot,
8 and those who are in the flesh cannot please God.
9a But you are not in the flesh; you are in the Spirit,
 b since the Spirit of God dwells in you.
 c Anyone who does not have the Spirit of Christ does not belong to him.
10a But if Christ is in you,
 b though the body is dead because of sin, the spirit is life because of righteousness.
11a If the Spirit of him who raised Jesus from the dead dwells in you,
 b he who raised Christ from the dead will give life to your mortal bodies also through his Spirit that dwells in you.
12 So then, brothers and sisters, we are debtors, not to the flesh, to live according to the flesh —
13a for if you live according to the flesh, you will die;
 b but if by the Spirit you put to death the deeds of the body, you will live.

*14 For all who are led by the Spirit of God are children of God.
15a For you did not receive a spirit of slavery to fall back into fear,
 b but you have received a Spirit of adoption. When we cry, "Abba! Father!"
16 it is that very Spirit bearing witness with our spirit that we are children of God,
17a and if children, then heirs,
 b heirs of God and joint heirs with Christ —
 c if, in fact, we suffer with him so that we may also be glorified with him.*

On the peculiar construction within Romans 7:24-8:1 see our second chapter, pp. 35-37.

The first person singular, the famous "I" of Romans 7, has completely disappeared in Romans 8:1-17. There is but one singular, a second person ("has set *you* free," v. 2), but elsewhere, besides the third person, the chapter has always the second or first person plural. In verse 12 Paul addresses his readers with "brothers [and sisters]." There are no longer rhetorical questions, no diatribe style. Paul reasons and argues; he draws conclusions and points to the inevitable implications of the life according to the Spirit.

Romans 8 is called the chapter of the Spirit. While in Romans 1-7 the term "spirit" occurs but five times and in Romans 9-16 but eight times, *pneuma* ("Spirit" or "spirit") is used in Romans 8 in verses 2, 4, 5 (twice), 6, 9 (three times), 10, 11 (twice), 13, 14, 15 (twice), 23, 26 (twice) and 27. Almost always the Spirit of God is meant. Two or three times Paul writes about the human spirit: see in verse 15 the first *pneuma* and in verse 16 the second; in verse 10, it could be God's Spirit, although, more likely, our spirit is intended, that is, we ourselves insofar we are under the influence of God's Spirit.

In Romans 8:2 we have the opposition between Spirit

and sin (literally: between "the law of the Spirit of life in Christ Jesus" and "the law of sin and of death"). From verse 3 onwards, however, it becomes clear that the law is weak and the "flesh" enters the scene. The whole pericope 8:1-17 is dominated by another opposition, namely that between Spirit and "flesh": see verses 4, 12 and 15, and compare verse 5a with 5b, verse 6a with 6b, verses 7-8 with 9-11 and verse 13a with 13b.

The style of 8:1-17 is intriguing. Paul writes in an objective *proclaiming* style. Christians must know and had better realize that Jesus' death and resurrection have brought them life (see the past tenses in vv. 2, 3, 11 and 15), that they no longer are "according to the flesh" or "in the flesh" (see vv. 5, 8 and 9) and that the Spirit, or Christ, dwells in them (see vv. 9, 10, 11 and 15). All this is given them by way of information. However the style is also *exhortative*. Christians can no longer "live according to the flesh" (very clearly in vv. 12-13). One could therefore call the real change effected by the Christ event — of which the presence of the Spirit is the result — only a somewhat provisional or still incomplete victory. There remains the possibility that Christians do not live according to their new status. Apparently, in a first function, the description of "the life according to the flesh" calls attention to the manner in which Christians have lived in an unregenerate state. One must be duly informed. Nonetheless this description is intended, above all, to avert the danger that still threatens every Christian. The message that we are in Christ and have the Spirit is the basis for exhortation and is, in a certain sense, itself already admonition and warning.

The Line of Thought

In Romans 8:1-17 we can distinguish three subunits: verses 1-4, 5,11 and 12-17.

a) *God sets us free through his Son* (vv.1-4). The first subunit elaborates what has already been mentioned in 7:24b-25a. The expressions "([from] now [on] no condemnation" (v. 1), "has set you free" (v. 2) and "God condemned sin" (v. 3) are, regarding content, connected with "to rescue" in 7:24b. In 8:1-3 the deliverance of the Christian "from the law of sin and of death," as well as "the condemnation of sin in the flesh," is attributed to God himself. God has effected this by sending his Son Jesus Christ in a flesh similar to our sinful flesh. All this constitutes a lengthy answer to the question of 7:24b and, at the same time, a development of the short thanksgiving in 7:25a.

Through the purpose clause of verse 4 (*hina*, "so that") another idea comes to the forefront. What God in his saving act really intends is the fulfillment by Christians of what is required by the law. They should no longer walk according to the flesh but according to the Spirit.

b) *Flesh and Spirit* (vv. 5-11). Twice in verses 5-6, by means of parallel clauses, life according to the flesh is opposed to life according to the Spirit. Verses 7-8, then, indicate that "those who are in the flesh" cannot please God. Until verse 8 Paul speaks mainly in the third person, in a general and arguing way. In verse 9ab, somewhat abruptly, he addresses his readers: "But you are not in the flesh; you are in the Spirit, since the Spirit of God dwells in you." The negative verse 9c is again general: "Anyone who does not have the Spirit of Christ does not belong to him." In verses 10-11, however, the second person plural recurs.

Verses 7-8 deal briefly with being in the flesh, verses 9-11 more extensively with being in the Spirit. In verses 9-11 this thought is developed in a rather jerky way. This can be developed as follows:

– Because God's Spirit dwells in us, we are in the Spirit (v. 9ab).
– Because we possess Christ's Spirit, we belong to him (v. 9c expresses this negatively).
– Because Christ is in us, we live through righteousness (v. 10).
– Because God's Spirit who raised Jesus dwells in us, God will raise our mortal bodies through the indwelling Spirit (v. 11).

The last verse concludes the small unit of verses 9-11. In it not only God, Christ and Spirit are mentioned, but there are also the three temporal dimensions: the past saving deed, the present indwelling of the Spirit, the future resurrection life.

c) *Children of God* (vv. 12-17). Verse 11 is a conclusion. We must, however, connect verses 12-17 with what precedes. Verse 12 draws the conclusion from what is emphatically put forward in verses 9-11. Because we are in the Spirit, we must live according to the Spirit. We have already indicated Paul's somewhat unusual way of reasoning. The fact that God's Spirit dwells in us does not make us immune. The danger remains that we may live according to the flesh. In verse 13a this negative possibility is dealt with and death is mentioned as a result of such a way of life. Verse 13b, on the other hand, is admonitory: "if by the Spirit you put to death the deeds of the body, you will live."

From verse 14 onwards Paul is again describing the regenerate existence of the Christian, now by means of the idea of "sonship." In verse 17 this leads to the perspective of the still future state of being joint heirs with Christ. This includes eschatological glory. Suffering with Christ is, however, its condition. Then, in verse 18, Paul utters his conviction that our sufferings on earth do not begin to equal that glorification. According to verse 28, all things (thus also suffering) work for good for those who love God. Ultimately, they will be glorified (see v. 30).

The Indwelling Spirit

The frequent appearance of "Spirit" in this passage proves it to be a key concept. It must have been clear to the readers: God has set free the "I" from a hopeless, wretched situation; God acted by sending his Son in the flesh and condemning sin; with the result that God's Spirit now dwells in Christians. Thus a new "Christian" way of life becomes possible.

A number of things strike us with regard to Christ and the Spirit in Romans 8:1-17.

(1) In verses 1 and 2 there are the expressions "those who are in *Christ Jesus*" and "life *in Christ Jesus*." In verse 10, however, we meet the opposite expression: "Christ *in you*."

(2) In verse 9a we read "you are *in the Spirit*" and in verses 9b, 11a and 11b, again, the opposite phrase: "the Spirit of God dwells *in you*."

(3) The same verse 9 speaks of "the Spirit *of God*" (see also v. 11: "the Spirit of him who raised Jesus from the dead"), but also of "a Spirit *of Christ*" (see also v. 15: "the Spirit of adoption").

(4) Within verses 8 and 9 there is the opposition of being "in the Spirit" and being "in the flesh," and in verses 4 and 5 that of living "according to the Spirit" and living "according to the flesh" (see also v. 13).

(5) In verses 13 and 14 we also have "*by* the Spirit" (v. 13: *dia*, and v. 14: an instrumental dative).

It is common knowledge that in his letters Paul makes frequent usage of the expressions "in Christ, in the Lord, in the Spirit," but rarely does he use the corresponding formula: Christ, the Lord, the Spirit in us. Reading Romans 8:1-2 one immediately is confronted with the formulaic character of "in Christ." What does Paul mean here by this expression? A careful consideration of the opposition Spirit-flesh in Romans 8 may help us in our quest.

In the light of 8:2-3 and 11 there can be no doubt that deliverance from sin, to which the flesh had been sold, occurred through Jesus' death on the cross and his resurrection. For the Christian this liberation becomes real in baptism. From that moment onwards the Christian is no longer in the flesh; he or she is in Christ and in the Spirit. "In" does, of course, not have a local meaning. We must understand that the Christian is no longer under the dominion of flesh and sin; the Christian lives under the influence of the Spirit. Moreover, Christians are led by the Spirit of God in such a real way that we should not be surprised that the expression can be inverted: not only are we in the Spirit, but the Spirit is and dwells in us. After all, in 7:17-20 the sin was also said to dwell in the "I," in the flesh.

In 8:16 Paul clearly distinguishes between Spirit and spirit: God's Spirit bears witness together with our spirit. The human spirit is not a higher "spiritual" principle, part of the human being. No, the spirit is the whole being, seen as conscious, knowing and willing. It remains quite remarkable that elsewhere in this pericope, with the exception of verse 15 and, perhaps, verse 10 ("your spirit"), Paul always speaks of the Spirit of God or Christ who is given to Christians and now dwells in them. There is no difference between the Spirit of God and the Spirit of Christ.

If we have the Spirit of Christ (v. 9), then Christ himself is in us (v. 10).

Finally, if being "in the Spirit" means that we are led by this Spirit, we can without difficulty assume that the frequent Pauline expression "in Christ" is (often) best understood as the equivalent of "led and driven by Christ." Perhaps we should paraphrase "being in Christ" as follows: our existence is determined and transformed by Christ's death and resurrection in an enduring manner. This transformation implies that Christ's indwelling Spirit makes us children of God and "heirs of God, joint heirs with Christ" (8:17).

Once again, all this is not just information. Being a new creation, having a really redeemed existence is also a call to a correspondingly new life, a life according to the Spirit, no longer according to the flesh.

II. Nothing can separate us from the love of God (Romans 8:31-39)

It would seem that Romans 8:31-39 functions not only as the conclusion of chapter 8 but also as th conclusion of the entire second section (chapters 5-8) of the long dogmatic segment, 1:18-11:36. The faith certainty of 5:1-11 is also present in 8:31-39. Although verses 31-39 continue the development of thought which was already introduced by verses 17-18, the introductory question, "What then are we to say about these things," of verse 31 marks a new beginning. The passage clearly ends with verse 39. In 9:1 a new section begins.

We will first discuss the structure of the text, then its

content. We conclude with a consideration of Paul's confidence of salvation.

A First Reading of the Text

a) *Diatribe style?*

The many (rhetorical) questions in verses 31-39 show that the quiet reasoning of verses 1-30 no longer continues. The first question, *ti oun eroumen* ... (v. 31a; see also 4:1; 6:1; 7:7; 9:14 and 30), clearly reminds us of the diatribe style, so prominent, for instance, in Romans 3. In the Pauline diatribe we can often distinguish a double (or threefold) question and a double answer; both the second (or third) question and the second answer usually determine and explain the first members. The questions present a difficulty or objection, a false inference or absurd reaction concerning Paul's preaching. The answers then bring Paul's (usually vehement) reply. See pp. 31-33.

Here, in 8:31-35, that pattern is broken. The first question does not raise an objection nor a false inference. Together with the following questions it is used to introduce a new consideration, a conclusion from the preceding statements. True, the second question (v. 31bc) specifies the first, but neither here nor after verse 32 is an explicit answer given. Otherwise than in Romans 3 and in diatribes in general, everything within 8:31-35 is in question form! The answers must be supplemented by the addressees; they are suggested by the rhetorical questions.

b) *Verses 33b and 34b*

Many exegetes, following the early Greek commentators, deny that every clause in verses 31-35 is a question. In their opinion verses 33b and 34b are statements, almost exclamations. Some would translate verses 33-34 as follows:

33a Who will bring any charge against God's elect?
  b [Nobody,] for it is God who justifies! (See, for instance, the NRSV.)
34a Who is to condemn?
  b [Nobody,] for it is Christ Jesus, who died, yes, who was raised, who is at the right hand of God, who indeed intercedes for us!

Others point to the judicial pair *dikaioô-katakrinô* ("to justify-to condemn") and connect verse 33b with verse 34a: "If it is God who justifies, who is to condemn?" A similar connection is found in Isaiah 50:8: "He who vindicates [= justifies] me is near. Who will contend with me [= condemn me]?" This Old Testament verse should be mentioned here since the passage Isaiah 50:7-9 (with its questions "who ... who ... who ...?") is probably at the background of Romans 8:33-34.

Yet, we ourselves prefer another punctuation (so already Augustine). In this alternative proposal verses 33b and 34b each repeat and determine the questions of verses 33a and 34a by adding a new one. We have thus in verse 33: "Who will bring any charge against God's elect? God who justifies, [will he lay a charge]?" The implied answer is: No! In verse 34 we have: "Who is to condemn? [Is it] Jesus who ...?" Again, the answer is implied: No! The same structure is present in verse 35.

c) *The structure*

The main question, which with its implicit answer "no one" functions almost as a thesis, is given in verse 31c: "Who is against us?" Three times it is repeated, in varied form, with the same "who":

"Who will bring any charge ...?" (v. 33a),
"Who is to condemn?" (v. 34a),
"Who will separate us ...?" (v. 35a).

Each of these questions is accompanied by a second one (vv. 33b, 34b and 35b). Each time the answer implied is "no." The verses 33-35 thus belong together.

Verse 36 contains an Old Testament citation, Psalm 44:23. The citation should prove the correctness of what Paul writes in verse 35. One can consider verses 37-39 as the explicit answer to the questions of verse 35. Moreover, verse 35 (questions) and verses 38-39 (answer) form an inclusion: note the common terms "to separate, love, Christ Jesus" and the two analogous lists. From all this it can be concluded that verses 36-39 belong to verse 35 and therefore also to verses 33-34.

Verse 32ab ("He who did not withhold his own Son, but gave him up for all of us") explains verse 31b ("if God is for us"). On the other hand verse 32c ("will he not with him also give us everything else?") agrees with verse 31c ("who is against us?"). Verses 31 and 32 clearly belong together.

In the light of this analysis it seems best to distinguish two units in 8:31-39, one long, the other short:

(a) verses 31-32, and
(b) verses 33-39.

Here follows the structured text:

(a) 31a What then are we to say about these things?
*   b   If God is for us,*
*   c   who is against us?*
*   32a   He who did withhold his own Son,*
*   b   but gave him up for all of us,*
*   c   will he not with him also give us everything else?*
(b) 33a Who will bring any charge against God's elect?
*   b   Is it God who justifies?*

34a Who is to condemn?
  b   Is it Christ Jesus,
          who died,
          yes, who was raised,
          who is at the right hand of God,
          who indeed intercedes for us?
35a Who will separate us from the love of Christ
  b   Will hardship, or distress, or persecution,
          or famine, or nakedness,
          or peril, or sword?
36   As it is written,
          "For your sake we are being killed all day long;
          we are accounted as sheep to be slaughtered"
          (Psalm 44:23).
37 No, in all these things we are more than conquerors through him who loved us.
38 For I am convinced that
          neither death, nor life,
          nor angels, nor rulers,
          nor things present, nor things to come,
          nor powers,
39   nor height, nor depth,
          nor anything else
    will be able to separate us from the love of God in Christ Jesus our Lord.

d) *Discussion*

In (a), the introductory "What then are we to say about these things?" (v. 31a) is followed by two parallel questions (v. 31c and v. 32c), each preceded by a conditional or relative clause (v. 31b and v. 32ab). We here distinguish two thoughts. (1) If God is for us, nobody against us can attain anything. (2) If God has given up his own Son, it can be assumed that God will give us all the rest.

In (b), we have three double questions. Each time the first is introduced by "who" (v. 33: God; v. 34: Christ; v. 35:

sufferings). Only the third double question (v. 35) which, moreover, is grounded by an Old Testament citation (v. 36), possesses an explicit answer: verses 37-39 (vv. 38-39 further explain v. 37). The second unit is carried by a threefold conviction: God will not accuse his elect; Christ will not condemn them; no creature can separate them from God's love.

In these units the greater length of verse 32 and of verses 35-39 respectively betray the *crescendo*, which builds to the climax at the end.

This entire passage is most probably Paul's own composition. It is better not to speak of a traditional hymn nor of a catechism-fragment with question and answer. In verses 33-35 Paul is influenced by Isaiah 50:7-9; in verse 36 he cites Psalm 44:23. In both verses 32 and 34 he takes up and edits earlier Christian tradition. In verses 38-39 he may have employed traditional expressions in his own free way. Nonetheless, the structure as well as the ideas are no doubt essentially Pauline. God's love and Christ's love are emphasized very much, even terminologically: see the expressions in verse 35 and at the end of verse 39; see also the verb "to love" with Christ as subject in verse 37. Paul is able to vary his language since for him the love of Christ does not differ from the love of God which is manifest in Christ Jesus.

Content

The structure is in function of the content. In his commentary, Ulrich Wilckens calls Romans 8:31-39 "the song of songs of the certainty of salvation" (*das Hohelied der Heilsgewissheit*). The text, he says, is characterized by an ascending intensity of language (a *gesteigerte sprachliche Intensität*, p. 177). That confidence is already present at the end of the preceding pericope:

> *For those whom he foreknew he also predestined to be conformed to the image of his Son, in order that he might be the firstborn within a large family. And those whom he predestined he also called; and those whom he called he also justified; and those whom he justified he also glorified (8:29-30).*

The past tense of the last verb ("glorified," that is, has already glorified) suggests that the final destination of Christians is already realized. The connected clauses of verses 29-30 give expression to Paul's deepest conviction and his rock-solid confidence of salvation. God will not forsake his Christians. He will lead them to their eschatological destiny. Immediately thereafter, in 8:31-35, Paul repeatedly emphasizes the certainty of faith by means of nine questions. At the end, in verses 37 and 38-39, the two solemn answers equally bring home that same conviction: nothing, no creature — not even if it be superhuman — will be able to separate us from the love of God.

Romans 8:31-39, however, is more than a triumphalistic ending. The pericope takes up the motifs which were not developed in verses 19-30. At the end of verse 17 Paul writes in a subordinate clause: "if, in fact, we suffer with him." In verse 18, he continues: "I consider that the sufferings of this present time are not worth comparing with the glory about to be revealed to us." We must assume that the phrase "all things" of verse 28 includes also these sufferings: "We know that all things work together for good for those who love God." In verse 32, the terms "not to withhold" and "to give up" point to the suffering of the Son. Finally, in verses 35 and 37-39, in a very explicit way, Paul emphasizes that no kind of suffering can separate us from the love of God. So it has become evident to all readers that Paul's statement of 8:1 ("There is therefore now no condemnation for those who are in Christ Jesus") does not mean that Christ's victory removes the possibility of suffering from Christians. Paul recognizes that in this life on earth faith co-exists with danger, persecution, strife and temptation.

Neither the expression of the certainty in faith nor the mention of suffering's provisional but positive place in life — however explicitly stated by commentators — fully translates Paul's intention. In all that Paul writes in Romans 8:31-39 there is a parenetical undertone. The manifold, insistent questioning invites the readers to agree. They should share in his faith conviction and take courage from it. By pointing to adversity Paul exhorts his fellow Christians to endurance and perseverance. There is exhortation, even when he writes: "... in all these things we are more than conquerors ...."

Certainty?

In Romans 8:17 Paul has dealt with the expected, though still future, glory of the Christians: "if, in fact, we suffer with Christ so that we may also be glorified with him." Is the last verb of 8:30 ("glorified") therefore perhaps a so-called "prophetic" past tense by which the confidence of what can be expected is highlighted? This would be strange since the other verbs with the same tenses are not prophetic. We may perhaps understand the verb "glorified" as follows: in principle God has already glorified Christians. Future, end-time glorification determines their present existence; it is anticipated in an already present Christian glory.

At any rate, the sentences of verses 29-30 very much suggest that everything, as far as God is concerned, is already decided and realized. Is there, according to Paul, a divine predestination which does not take human freedom into account? I do not think so, for these sentences function within the framework of faith confidence. Theo C. de Kruijf explains: "It is no intellectual manner of thought, but an expression of boundless confidence in the promise of God who 'knows' us (that is: has the most intimate relation with us) even before we are born ..." (p. 176).

Some exegetes take "glorified" of verse 30 in what they judge to be its most obvious sense. In their opinion Paul does not have in mind definitive salvation after death. He speaks of an already realized glorification during Christian life. Christians are children of God; they have the Spirit; they are "a new creation" (see 2 Cor 5:17 and Gal 6:15). Christians who "with unveiled faces" see the glory of the Lord "are being transformed ... from one degree of glory to another" through the working of the Spirit, already now, in this life (2 Cor 3:18). These exegetes do not deny the possible increase of that glory nor its completion at the resurrection. Nonetheless, they maintain that in Romans 8 Paul's attention is focused on the present glory in the regenerate existence of the Christian.

It seems to me that this interpretation is less correct. In 8:17 Paul clearly situates the glorification in the future. In verses 18-25 he speaks of the revelation of the glory, of hope, of the awaited adoption and of the redemption of the body. The whole passage is thus characterized by that eager expectation of our final salvation. In verse 11 Paul refers to the future resurrection of the mortal body through the indwelling Spirit. According to verse 23 the Spirit is precisely the *aparchê*, the "first fruits," not yet the eschatological fulfillment.

In view of all this, notwithstanding that strange past tense at the end of verse 30 ("glorified"), we may safely assume that in Romans 8 Paul is above all thinking of the still future definitive salvation, not in this earthly life but after death. This does, of course, not exclude the already present glory. On the contrary, this glory is the very basis on which hope, confidence and certainty are established.

One more remark should be made. In his discourse Paul not only declares and expresses his certainty; he also exhorts Christians to endurance. In this song of songs of certainty of salvation thanks to the faithfulness of *God*, there is also, underneath, uncertainty regarding the perseverance of *Christians*.

If God Is For Us ...

Paul's dependence on traditional Christian "creedal" language in verses 32 and 34 is undeniable: God did not withhold his own Son, but gave him up for us; Christ Jesus died, was raised and is at the right hand of God. Nor should one forget that Paul also uses the seven terms of the list of verse 35b (3 = 2 = 2) elsewhere in his letters in order to describe his own apostolic suffering (see 2 Cor 4:8-9; 6:4; 11:26-27; 12:10). Moreover, six of the seven terms in verse 35b frequently appear in the Septuagint, not only separately but also in various combinations. Most of these Old Testament passages present warnings of Yahweh (often through his prophets) and announcements of punishment. The individual, Israel as a whole and the nations: all will suffer hardships because they do not observe God's laws or commandments.

Paul radically transposes these Old Testament traditions. The terms no longer point to future calamity and punishment; rather they depict the inevitable suffering of Christians which is undergone in this age because of Jesus (see v. 36: according to Paul the phrase "for your sake" most probably refers to Christ). Yet, in the midst of all this suffering

Christians secure an overwhelming victory through that same Jesus who has loved them (see v. 37).

No doubt Paul in verse 35b mentions circumstances which are inimical forces and which could separate Christians from their Lord. A second list follows in verses 38-39. It deals with the totality of antagonism, rather than with one specific enemy, that could separate us from God. Nonetheless Aquinas' comment on the double term "neither death, nor life" is to the point: death is the *praecipuum inter terribilia* ("the most terrible") of the inimical forces, but life is the *praecipuum inter appetibilia* ("the most appealing"). From the generalizing verses 38-39 it appears that Paul sees behind these hardships super-human personal spirits (for instance, angels, principalities, powers; perhaps still other terms), and probably in the final analysis the great enemy Satan himself.

Yet, God is neither absent nor passive. The whole stage is allowed and even planned by God. He did not spare his own Son but gave him up for all of us (see vv. 31-32). God also consents to (or has arranged) the necessary likeness between Christ and Christians: if they want to be glorified with Christ, they must suffer with him (see vv. 29-30). It would seem that for Paul suffering is negative and dangerous. It could separate us from God's love; it must disappear in the eschaton. Yet, on earth, suffering cannot totally be avoided; it may even become redemptive and salvific (see 8:28).

As we have seen, the end of verse 30 looks forward to the future as certain: God has (already) glorified us. By means of it Paul underlines his conviction and his belief in God's invincible plan. God will bring to completion the work he once began (see Phil 1:6). The same vision controls 8:31-39. If God was for us in the past — and the way he acted in

Christ has sufficiently demonstrated this —, he will be for us in the future. So nothing will be able to separate us from the love of God in Christ Jesus!

However, the tone in verses 31-39 is different from that in verses 28-30. In verses 31-39 Paul takes into account the "not yet" of the Christian condition. We have already seen that Paul comes back to the theme of suffering present in verses 17-18. To be sure, in verses 31-34 the future perspective is still that of the eschaton, the judgment day. The future tenses of verses 35 and 39 ("will separate" and "will be able to separate") are, nonetheless, no longer merely eschatological: Christ is pleading our cause (see end of v. 34, present); afflictions are present (see v. 35b); "we are being killed all day long" (v. 36). Yet victory is already ours within this very real situation of troubles and tribulation (see v. 37). Anticipated eschatology, however, should engender neither contempt for mundane realities, nor neglect of daily responsibilities.

CHAPTER SEVEN

Creation Which Groans (Romans 8:19-22)

The third chapter of Vatican II's pastoral constitution *Gaudium et spes* ("The Church in the Modern World") discusses human activity during this earthly life and highlights its lasting character. At the end of time, at the resurrection of the dead, "While charity and its fruits endure, all that creation which God made on man's account will be unchained from the bondage of vanity" (*GS*, 39, in *The Documents of Vatican II*, ed. W.M. Abbott, New York: 1966, p. 237). This statement contains a clear reference to 1 Corinthians 13:8: "Love never ends" (see also v. 13), and to Romans 8:21: "creation itself will be set free from its bondage to decay." What of "creation" will remain and what will disappear?

In Romans 12:2 after "Do not be conformed to this world" (literally: Do not be conformed to this *age*) one would expect "but transform this world." Paul, however, writes in the passive: "but be transformed by the renewing of our minds, so that you may discern what is the will of God — what is good and acceptable and perfect." This verse provides us with a twofold insight. For Paul this world is not simply the gift of God's good creation. Our world is alienated from God. Furthermore, for Paul, a life pleasing to God first supposes the reformation of the inner being of a person. We have to wonder what role creation plays in this regard and to what fate the world is destined.

This seventh chapter of our book is a biblical reflection on what Paul refers to as "the whole creation ... groaning in labor pains" (Rom 8:22) and its future. May we attach a lasting, "eternal" value to the realizations of humanity in creation, to production and culture? To what extent, according to Scripture, is humanity obliged to keep creation sound, and to what degree does the Bible share in ecological concerns? For what does our Christian hope guarantee continuity? These and similar questions form the subject of this chapter. In the first and second parts, however, no general overview of the biblical vision of the world is offered. We prefer a careful reading of one key passage, Romans 8:19-22, within its context, 8:18-30. However, the questions raised will direct our inquiry and will be dealt with more explicitly in the third part.

I. Train of thought

In regard to the place of verses 18-30 within Romans 8 we may refer to our discussion in the preceding chapter: see p. 94. This is the text:

18 I consider that the sufferings of this present time are not worth comparing with the glory about to be revealed to us.
19 For the creation waits with eager longing for the revealing of the children of God;
20 for the creation was subjected to futility, not of its own will but by the will of the one who subjected it, in hope
21 that the creation itself will be set free from its bondage to decay and will obtain the freedom of the glory of the children of God.
22 We know that the whole creation has been groaning in labor pains until now;
23 and not only the whole creation, but we ourselves, who have the first fruits of the Spirit, groan inwardly while we wait for adoption, the redemption of our bodies.

24 For in hope we were saved. Now hope that is seen is not hope. For who hopes for what is seen?
25 But if we hope for what we do not see, we wait for it with patience.
26 Likewise the Spirit helps us in our weakness; for we do not know how to pray as we ought, but that very Spirit intercedes with sighs too deep for words.
27 And God, who searches the heart, knows what is the mind of the Spirit, because the Spirit intercedes for the saints according to the will of God.
28 We know that all things work together for good for those who love God, who are called according to his purpose.
29 For those whom he foreknew he also predestined to be conformed to the image of his Son, in order that he might be the firstborn within a large family.
30 And those whom he predestined he also called; and those whom he called he also justified; and those whom he justified he also glorified.

The Textual Unit

In Romans 8, verses 18 to 30 can be taken as a unit. Verse 18 and verses 28-30 frame this entire text. In verse 18 Paul writes: "I consider that the sufferings of this present time are not worth comparing with the glory that is to be revealed to us." Verse 18 is more than a transitional verse. With its solemn formulation, this verse stands as a thesis in regard to what follows, but it also connects, in terms of content, with the end of verse 17: we share in Christ's sufferings, and likewise in his glory. The main thought of verse 18 is concerned with the fact that suffering is not comparable with glory. That thought, however, is not further developed unless we say that the sufferings are not comparable since they are short; they are a token of the end (vv. 19-27), and they work for good (vv. 28-30). In reality it is not suffering but glory that gets the attention, more specifically, the ardent, impatient looking forward to the revelation of the glory.

Verses 28-30 decidedly possess a certain independence. They describe God's lasting faithfulness. Still, there is sufficient reason to attach these verses to the preceding argument. With the conclusion of verse 30, "God glorified," we are once again reminded of the theme of the (future) glory which verses 17, 18 and 21 had expressed. With "Son" and "family" (literally: brethren), verse 29 is connected with verses 14-17; likewise, reflections about "Son, family, possession of the Spirit" are clearly present in verses 28-30, as well as in the passage as a whole (see "Son" in v. 29, "adoption, family, children" in vv. 19, 21, 23 and 29, and "Spirit" in vv. 26-27). A third common theme is found in verse 28; like verses 17 and 18, it also speaks about the adversities of this life.

Content

In Romans 8:18-30 it is best to distinguish four smaller divisions. After the title verse, verses 19-22 develop a single idea. The creation which was unwillingly subjected to futility and will be freed from bondage and decay looks longingly toward the glory and revealed freedom of the children of God.

The second section, verses 23-25, is hardly a closed unity. The transition is grammatically harsh. Verse 23 is still somewhat dependent on the verb "know that" with which verse 22 began: "We know that the whole creation has been groaning in labor pains until now; and not only the creation, but we ourselves ...." Further, verses 24-25 form a small digression about precisely what "hope" means. While verses 19-22 had been about creation, verses 23-25 deal with believers ("we"). Notwithstanding this unevenness, one can still point out several more or less equivalent terms:

Verses 19-22	*Verses 23-25*
19: waits ... for	23: we wait for
	25: we wait for
20: creation	23: bodies
20: hope	24-25: hope-hope
21: will be set free	23: redemption
21: children of God	23: adoption
22: groaning creation	23: we ourselves... groan

At the end of verse 25, after the excursus about hope, Paul returns to his train of thought with "we wait for" (see the same verb in vv. 23 and 19).

Verses 26-27 constitute the third small unity. After the interruption of verses 24-25, the argument is carried further. In verse 26a it is said that the Spirit helps us in our weakness. The Spirit who dwells within us is meant (see vv. 9-11, 12-16, and especially v. 23: we have already received the Spirit as "first fruits"). Verses 26b-27 then explain in what the assistance consists, namely, in praying with sighs too deep for words. For what does the Spirit pray? Probably we must answer from verses 19 and 20: in order that the future glory of the children of God might be speedily revealed. Besides that of the creation and ourselves, there is a third instance of eager awaiting and longing, that of the Spirit. "Likewise" at the beginning of verse 26 joins the similar thought from the start of verse 23: "not only the creation, but we ourselves." The "sighs" of the Spirit differ from ours. The Spirit pleads according to God's will. The wordless sighs of the Spirit are a help for our weakness and ignorance. In Christians there is a lack of insight and ability. It is as if the words we use are inadequate. The Spirit, on the other hand, does not need words.

The fourth section, verses 28-30, no longer deals with a subjective looking forward. Through the insight that Christians have into the faithfulness of God who foreknows, who predestines, calls, justifies, and glorifies, they can objectively deduce that the present-day sufferings (v. 28; see vv. 17-18) are, for those whom God has called, whom God loves, a way to good. Such sufferings work for good; they promote salvation.

II. Explanation

In Romans 8:18-30 Paul is involved in a reasoning process. Not only does he use a variety of arguments, but even his style is argumentative (see the particle *gar*, "for," which occurs seven times in this passage [vv. 18, 19, 20, 22, 24a and c, 26]). Also striking are the expressions and definitions within verses 24-25 and the "golden chain" (*catena aurea*) which is formed by the enumeration in verses 29-30. Further, Paul three times introduces an utterance with the help of a verb which underscores his conviction: "I consider" in verse 18, and "we know" in verse 22 and once again in verse 28. The vocabulary and the images possess an apocalyptic character, especially in verses 19-23. We refer to expressions like "the present time," "the [future] glory," "revelation," the "groaning" of creation and the messianic, eschatological woes. A second reading will offer us an opportunity to give the necessary attention to some exegetical difficulties.

Verses 18-22

18 I consider that the sufferings of this present time are not worth comparing with the glory about to be revealed to us.

19 For the creation waits with eager longing for the revealing of the children of God;
20 for the creation was subjected to futility, not of its own will but by the will of the one who subjected it, in hope
21 that the creation itself will be set free from its bondage to decay and will obtain the freedom of the glory of the children of God.
22 We know that the whole creation has been groaning in labor pains until now;

The expression "this present time" is the translation of *ho nyn kairos* (literally: "the moment of now," see 3:26; 11:5 and 2 Cor 8:14). The "present time" is not the whole of human history. Probably intended is the period of time which began with the gospel events and will be terminated by the Parousia. Paul thinks concretely of the time in which he and his fellow believers live. That time will not endure much longer. In Romans 13:11-12, Paul writes: "... you know what time it is, how it is now the moment for you to wake from sleep. For salvation is nearer to us now than when we became believers; the night is far gone, the day is near ...." Paul expects the speedy return of Jesus. He lives in a state of high expectation (compare the German term *Naherwartung*).

One can assume that Christians are already in the possession of glory; a glory, however, which must still be revealed. This will indeed occur as a profound transformation of Christians. The "revealing of the children of God" (v. 19) one must suppose as "their public presentation upon the universal scene" (Theo C. de Kruijf, p. 173), a sort of manifestation in the presence of, and being beheld by, the whole of creation. With the term "creation" in verses 19-22, Paul is thinking, we presume, of the created reality of this world (matter, plants, animals, and heavenly bodies); humanity is not included here. Paul personifies this creation: it suffers, it has human feelings and desires. In verse 19 the clause "waits with eager longing" translates the Greek term *apokaradokia*. In the Bible it is used only by Paul, here and in Philippians 1:20. One may suppose that Paul coined this compound term. "Futility" in verse 20 refers to a senseless, powerless and idle existence. This futility differs perhaps from the "bondage to decay" in verse 21, which then has a negative and pejorative meaning. "Bondage to decay" includes dissolution and death; it is contrary to immortality and glory.

It is preferable to regard God, rather than Satan or Adam, as the logical subject of "was subjected" in verse 20. Through the punitive decision of God, the whole of creation shares in the human situation after the Fall. Thus Pauline (and Jewish) anthropology sees it. The expression "not of its own will" (v. 20) and also perhaps the groaning and labor pains (v. 21) show, nevertheless, that in Paul's conception creation itself has not sinned. Its condition is unnatural. All of creation groans together and suffers travail. Creation waits for its liberation, which will coincide with that of Christians, but it will merely participate in the liberation. According to Paul, therefore, creation is not authentically independent, not authentically subsistent.

Verses 23-25

23 *and not only the whole creation, but we ourselves, who have the first fruits of the Spirit, groan inwardly while we wait for adoption, the redemption of our bodies.*
24 *For in hope we were saved. Now hope that is seen is not hope. For who hopes for what is seen?*
25 *But if we hope for what we do not see, we wait for it with patience.*

In verse 23, much emphasis is placed on "we;" "not only the creation, but we ourselves ... groan inwardly." This "we" is Paul and his addressees, the Christians of Rome. Because these Christians possess the Spirit as firstfruits, they can "groan inwardly" in their prayer and can anticipate adoption. Just as the already-possessed glory must become public (see vv. 19 and 21), so also Christians look forward to (the manifestation of) a "sonship," an adoption that is an already present reality, an actually existing way of life (see v. 15). It remains somewhat strange that in verse 23 adoption (literally: "sonship") is presented as a still future eschatological reality.

The expression "the redemption of our bodies" should not be thought of as a liberation of the soul from the body. The body itself must be freed from the bondage to decay to which it has been delivered up on account of sin. "There exist on the basis of God's plan of creation only corporeal human beings. And there will exist in God's plan of redemption also nothing but corporeal human beings" (Hendrik Baarlink, p. 126).

In verse 24a Paul expresses the tension between "the already" and the "not yet"; we are saved in such a way that we still must hope. "Hope that is seen" in verse 24b means hope for which the fulfillment is seen. One must no longer hope for a visible fulfilled hope (see v. 24c)! After the conditional protasis "but if we hope for what we do not see" in verse 25 follows "(then) we wait for it with patience." This conclusion is at the same time also a stimulus: we must persevere in our anticipation.

Verses 26-27

26 Likewise the Spirit helps us in our weakness; for we do not know how to pray as we ought, but that very Spirit intercedes with sighs too deep for words.
27 And God, who searches the heart, knows what is the mind of the

> *Spirit, because the Spirit intercedes for the saints according to the will of God.*

Not everything in these two verses is equally certain. The *syn* in the double compound verb *syn-anti-lambanetai* does not mean "together with (us);" here it has a strengthening function. The Spirit undeniably comes to help our weakness. The expression "as we ought" must be understood in the light of "according to the will of God" in verse 27: "as we ought" is "as God wills." The phrase "God who searches the hearts" is a biblical thought (see, for example, 1 Sam 16:7; 1 Kings 8:39; Ps 7:10 [9, ET]; Prov 15:11; Jer 17:9-10). God (= the Father) is indicated thereby. God knows what his Spirit, who is present in Christians, intends.

What does that Spirit do? Some exegetes think that Paul in verses 26-27 points to what occurs in heaven. According to this opinion the Spirit acts as helper of the saints in heaven. These exegetes refer to the "unspeakable" (*arrêtos*) words which Paul, caught up into Paradise, heard (see 2 Cor 12:4). This interpretation, however, seems far-fetched. Nor, most likely, should one think of the audible speech in tongues on earth, the inarticulate cries of the so-called "glossolalia," which ecstatic Christians practice in the Spirit (see 1 Cor 14). No, according to verses 26-27 the Spirit himself pleads with "unspoken" (*alalêtos*) groaning. His sighs do not need words; they are attentive to God's very will and thus intercede for the saints.

Verses 28-30

> 28 *We know that all things work together for good for those who love God, who are called according to his purpose.*
> 29 *For those whom he foreknew he also predestined to be conformed to the image of his Son, in order that he might be the firstborn within a large family.*

30 And those whom he predestined he also called; and those whom he called he also justified; and those whom he justified he also glorified.

In verse 28, as in verse 26, the *syn* in the compound verb (here *syn-ergei*) has probably a strengthening function: the verb thus signifies not simply "cooperating with someone" (for instance, God), but really "helping, furthering." Some, however, are of the opinion that the prefix is weakened so that the sense of the compound verb does not differ from the simple form.

The chain reasoning of verses 29-30 should supply the proof of the thesis which verse 28 had expressed: everything, including suffering, works to the good of those who love God; they are called according to his purpose. God's plan is great. God has the power to fulfill it. This fulfillment includes five stages:

(1) Those whom he foreknew
    (2) he also predestined;
(2) those whom he predestined
    (3) he also called;
(3) those whom he called
    (4) he also justified;
(4) those whom he justified
    (5) he also glorified.

The well-known *catena aurea* is perhaps a prepauline tradition. If so, then verse 29bc is an insertion, a Pauline addition: "to be conformed to the image of his Son, in order that he might be the firstborn within a large family." Indeed, Paul also speaks elsewhere of being conformed to Jesus Christ (see Phil 3:21), of the Son as "likeness" and "image" (see 2 Cor 3:18 and 4:4) and of the Son as first of those risen (see 1 Cor 15:20 and 23; compare 1 Col 1:18).

Perhaps the "Son" in the expression "the image of his Son" is an explanatory genitive with this nuance: the image which the Son himself is. The Son is the image of God (see 2 Cor 4:4). We are thus conformed to the visible form of the Father.

The past tense of "to glorify" at the end of verse 30 has already been discussed in our sixth chapter, see pp. 108-111.

III. THE FUTURE OF THE WORLD

In Romans 8:18-30 there is placed in the foreground a problem that Paul also discusses elsewhere (see, for example, Rom 5:3-5 and 2 Cor 1:3-11) and that apparently greatly engrossed him. How is it to be explained that those who are justified, who already possess the Spirit, still live amidst sufferings? What is the meaning and the function of those vicissitudes? Paul's answer in Romans 8 contains three elements. There is no comparison between the present sufferings and the future glory (v. 18); the future glory is near at hand (see the impatient "groans" in vv. 19-27); and, in seeming contradiction, these so negative sufferings accomplish salvation (vv. 28-30).

In this third section our attention is drawn to another problem, that of the cosmic dimension of the redemption (see especially vv. 19-22). Five questions serve to focus the problem. (1) How does Paul come to ascribe to the "sub-human" creation such human sentiments, desires and expressions? (2) How precisely does Paul see the relation between creation and human beings (Christians) and, how should we, in terms of our modern philosophy, view the relation between matter and spirit? (3) Whether or not "futility" (v. 20) and "bondage to decay" (v. 21) mean exactly the same, it is in any case Paul's idea that creation has been brought to an unnatural condition because of the sin of Adam. What do the natural sciences have to say about this? (4) Paul thought of a sort of deliverance and redemption of creation. Can we ourselves relate to this conviction? If so, is there a continuity between the present time and that which is to come? (5) Does the human stake in making the world habitable and in conquering space have a lasting, eschatological significance? And this not only for our personal salvation but also for that of the world: is there a future for that world? We begin with the first three questions.

Does Creation Groan?

We may not lose sight of the fact that Romans 8:19-22 possesses little independence. The sentence which began in verse 22 speaks of the subhuman creation; in verse 23 it spontaneously moves to a consideration about Christians. We must keep in mind the fact that Paul in Romans 8:19-30 is thinking, in the first place, of "the situation of the Christian still oppressed by suffering" (Anton Vögtle, "Röm. 8,19-22," p. 365). Paul is of the opinion that the suffering of Christians belongs to the eschatological woes which announce the nearness of the end. Thus he intends, and is able, to comfort and encourage his fellow Christians. The small subdivision about creation (vv. 19-22) functions merely as a step in the argument which deals with the sufferings, and has as such a somewhat accidental character. In regard to the questions that have been raised, that is not simply a loss. This lack of intentionality is, as it were, a guarantee of the authenticity of the ideas which merely make an incidental appearance. Vögtle, in our opinion, goes too far when he asserts that Paul does not at all want to inform his readers "about the fate of creation in the past, present and future" (p. 366).

a) *Personification*

In the Old Testament the connection between human beings and subhuman creation is essential. In the fate of nature, that of men and women is reflected. There is a kind of solidarity between nature and human beings. However, it might be asked whether the description of what happens in the cosmos is but a stylistic means to point out what occurs in the human person. I do not think so, for mythic conceptions still cling to Old Testament, often apocalyptic, texts about nature.

Paul personifies creation. He portrays it as a living, human reality, a person. To what extent has Paul, just as have the people of the Old Testament, considered part of lifeless creation as really "animated" and "living"? This is difficult to ascertain, but one may assume that Paul was a person of his time in this regard. Further, to which insight or experience does he refer with "we know" in verse 22? Do the "groaning" and "labor pains" of creation point only to a conviction he has gained from the Bible (see Gen 3:14-19: "in pain you shall bring forth children," v. 16; "cursed is the ground because of you," v. 17)? He probably also likewise relies on more concrete events which can be observed by his fellow Christians, for example, natural disasters such as earthquakes and floods or famines. Nonetheless, a precise answer to this complex question is difficult.

b) *The creation and the Christian*

According to Paul, redemption hardly means alienation or annihilation of the body and the material. Paul's vision is radically opposed to one of the philosophical and religious axioms of the Greeks and the gnostics. For them, that which is material is inferior and evil. Christians, on the contrary, await the resurrection of the body. The body will be changed, transformed. Just how this glorified condition can be more specifically described is not the main point here.

Not only for the body, but also for the whole created world, there is a future. In one way or another, the world will share in the glory of the children of God. With a striking emphasis, Paul unites the future of the world with that of the children of God: "the creation waits with eager longing for the revealing of the children of God" (v. 19); "the creation itself will be set free from its bondage and will obtain the freedom of the glory of the children of God" (v. 21). Indeed, the bondage of creation has come upon it as a consequence of the sin of Adam (see v. 20). Paul thus believed in a future, new, glorified world thanks to the glory of Christians. Walther Bindemann rightly concludes from this that such a vision forbids both demonization (*Verteufelung*) and divinization (*Vergöttlichung*) of the world.

Paul obviously possesses a belief in God as creator of heaven and earth. In the foreground, however, stands his Christian conviction, his belief that through and in Christ redeemed human beings are children of God and that their glory will be manifested. Paul's belief in redemption thus directs his thinking about creation. Romans 8:19-22 allows us to see more definitely how Paul understands the fate of creation united to that of redeemed humanity, and how redemption itself extends even as far as creation. The contemporary, philosophically trained Christian sympathizes with this magnificent Pauline idea.

c) *The creation without sin*

One can hardly suppose that Paul worried much about the question of what the situation of the material world would have been without the Fall, or precisely what effect the Fall had on nature. In Romans 8:19-22, with the expressions "subjected to futility" (a senseless existence) and "bondage to decay" (to corruption), Paul says in the first place that the world has been wounded through the sin of humanity. One need not deny that Paul, based on Genesis 3:17-19, really believed that through sin both humanity and nature were punished: death, decay, corruption, suffering. These are all "givens," of which one must say today that they still would exist regardless of the presence or absence of sin. One who fundamentalistically and biblically seeks an agreement between Romans 8:19-22 and the modern scientific-evolutionary world image is certainly on the wrong track.

Rupture or Union?

The last two questions concern the continuity between time and eternity: does such a continuity exist? Already in the case of humanity we come to a paradox. Christians work out their salvation in this present time, in and with their bodies. The resurrection of the body is awaited in hope. Yet, even in the present, there exist not only suffering and sickness, decay and death, but, notwithstanding all that, the assurance that precisely in the sufferings and the breakdown of earthly existence, in a paradoxical way, real life begins. "So we do not lose heart. Even though our outer nature is wasting away, our inner nature is being renewed day by day. For this slight momentary affliction is preparing us for an eternal weight of glory beyond all measure"

(2 Cor 4:16-17). What then is the place of God's creation, the subhuman world? Can something more be brought forward than a warning against possible misunderstandings? For misunderstandings do exist.

The "groaning of creation" is merely a personification or a remainder of mythic thought. It is wrong to understand the world as having its own significance, apart from humanity. The world exists for human beings; it was also punished along with human beings; its future is only a participation in the redemption of human beings, of Christians. "Without the redemption of humanity there could be no redemption of the body, and consequently even less redemption of the universe" (Stanislas Lyonnet, "Rédemption," p. 61). One cannot escape the impression that extreme ecologists may become worshippers of nature. They sound as if the world has value of itself, without humanity, and as if nature possesses a proper, absolute importance. Some even idolize and "resacralize" nature.

It is also wrong to think that the future glory will be the fruit of a continuing evolution, the result of an internal process, of sheer human effort. The paradox referred to above applies not only to humanity, but by analogy also to the surrounding world. The well-known New Testament scholar Heinrich Schlier puts it thus: not evolution, but God's surprising, overwhelming gift. He cautions against an openness to the world which may too easily become accommodation to the world (see "Das, worauf alles wartet," p. 605).

The naive idea of an unbroken continuity can thus not be accepted, but even less so that of radical discontinuity or absolute forsaking of the world. Just as the future glory of the risen body is entirely God's gift, but at the same time human work brought to completion in bodily existence, so will the new world surely be a world transformed by God, but certainly also the world as it has been in the course of time controlled and inhabited, placed in service, enriched and built up by many generations of humans. "From the fact that the redemption of the body extends to the entire universe, it follows that human labor — the efforts of man to master the material universe, to search out its mysteries, to domesticate and utilize it, to transform brute matter into instruments of greater and greater perfection, even to 'electronic brains' capable of operations that defy the intelligence of even the one who constructs them — all of human labor acquires an eternal value" (Lyonnet, "Rédemption," p. 60).

The Commission

All the above-mentioned misunderstandings must be corrected, but a thoroughly positive approach to creation is still demanded. According to Genesis 1:26-30, humankind, "as created in the image of God," receives from God the commission to populate the earth and subdue it. Cornelis Houtman says that we may idealize neither the Genesis image of God nor that of the human being as "image of God": "The image of God that is summoned up by 'image of God' is obviously not that of God who surrounds all of creation with concern and devotion, but the image of God as the one who, with power, acts against chaos," and humanity becomes "through the qualification 'image of God' typified as a sort of vice-regent, the extended hand of God on earth. His style of acting must be like that of an ideal king: he must make short work of all that threatens life ..." (p. 34 and pp. 31-32). Here in Genesis the Bible stresses in authoritative manner the unique place of human beings who have a task in respect to the created world.

How nature must remain healthy and the world habitable is nevertheless more a question of human thinking than of biblical revelation. The necessary preservation of nature, the viability of the cosmos, the legitimate ecological nature-loving condition: all of this belongs in full to the responsible activity of human beings. Human beings must live with nature, but they must also plan for their children's future. Therefore they will probably need to fight long and laboriously against environmental filth, contamination of the air and pollution of water. Modern people have begun to realize to what devastation of nature their inventions can lead. They will have to learn to live safely with nuclear reactors and atomic weapons. They and no one else are responsible for the environment of life and the wholeness of creation. Some might regard this as exaggerated anthropocentrism. But is responsible humanity not intended by God precisely as the center point and purpose of creation? We do not see how a so-called "eco-centrism" can better express the proper calling of human beings than a well-understood anthropocentrism.

In *Gaudium et spes*, the council fathers spoke optimistic, hopeful words: "Therefore, while we are warned that it profits a man nothing if he gain the whole world and lose himself, the expectation of a new earth must not weaken but rather stimulate our concern for cultivating this one .... For after we have obeyed the Lord, and in his Spirit nurtured on earth the values of human dignity, brotherhood and freedom, and indeed all the good fruits of our nature and enterprise, we will find them again, but freed of stain, burnished and transfigured. This will be so when Christ hands over to the Father a kingdom eternal and universal ... (*GS*, 39, in *Documents*, p. 237).

CHAPTER EIGHT

Critical and Actualizing Observations

Although in this book only two chapters from Paul's letter to the Romans are treated, no small difficulties have been encountered. Paul's ideas and reasoning are not always clear. What he says about the law, especially its relation to sin and the "flesh", is not easily grasped. To be sure, the law is holy and spiritual, but the same law is "weakened by the flesh" (Rom 8:2) and misused by sin. Through conscious transgression of the law sin becomes more sinful. Paul sometimes "plays" with the term law and give it different nuances. The personifications of sin in Romans 7 and of creature or nature in Romans 8 are rather unusual for modern readers. In both chapters there is also the Pauline concept "flesh," often in opposition to Spirit. What are its shades of meaning? Our search for the true identity of the "I" has been long and laborious, yet not without result. The same applies to the location in time of the conflict situation of the "I": before or after conversion? Further, how must we see and understand Paul's faith certainty of salvation? Another strange feature is the combination of proclamation and exhortation, of indicative and imperative. Sometimes we have the impression that the indicative itself already contains an imperative. During the course of this monograph it has become evident that Romans 7 and 8 require attentive study and, in regard to interpretation, often a delicate "weighing" of probable or possible proposals.

Two Considerations

The reading of these chapters spontaneously, as it were, takes into account the style genre which is characterized by rhetorical questions, personifications and dramatic representations. On two occasions, however, Paul seems to exaggerate in these chapters, at the risk of being misunderstood.

(1) The "I" is fleshly, is a slave, sold to sin; the "I" does not understand its own deeds; the "I" does what that very person hates and does not want to do. But — and this is, to be sure, the reader's healthy reaction — no human being is that bad; at least, nobody is permanently and always evil in such a way.

In Romans 7 we listen to the language of dramatic intensification and exaggeration. It would therefore be wrong to take its utterances in a literal sense. Exegetes, however, have done this. Referring to this Pauline text, they have spoken of the radical corruption of human nature, of a perversion of the human being to the very roots, of a so-called transsubjective sinful condition. The result is that, according to this view, all actions within the unregenerate state are the sinful manifestation and concretization of that condition. Even the striving for good and the keeping of the law are inevitably sin.

It would seem to me that such a picture of pre-Christian existence cannot appeal to what Paul, admittedly not without overstatement, works out in Romans 7.

(2) In Romans 8 also Paul appears to overdo his conviction. He underscores his faith certainty. Paul's arguing here is more than once introduced by "we know" or "I am convinced." He claims that there is no condemnation for those who are in Christ, that all things work for good, that God has predestined Christians to be conformed to the image of his Son, that God (already) has glorified them,

that nobody and nothing can separate them from the love of God in Christ Jesus.

Does final salvation, just as initial justification, depend on God's grace alone, not on human endeavor? Is there, according to Paul, after all a real divine predestination? Even today this view is defended, for example, in the otherwise valuable recent publication by Judith M. Gundry Volf, *Paul and Perseverance: Staying in and Falling Away* (WUNT 2/37; Tübingen, 1990).

In Romans 8 Paul is, again, exaggerating; his emphasis is no doubt one-sided. True, the faith certainty is grounded on what God has done for us and still will do, and on the conviction, too, that nothing is able to hinder God in his salvific plan. That certainty is repeatedly expressed and very much accentuated in Romans 8: in all adversities we have complete victory through God who loved us! Yet, notwithstanding these and similar enunciations, in Romans 8 we are also, implicitly but inescapably, given to understand that we Christians must live "according to the Spirit." Living a moral and religious life is by no means an automatic happening. Christians must collaborate with God's grace. Although this is not stated in so many words: Christians can lose their salvation through neglect and sin, through their own fault. Paul's confidence of salvation is a certainty of God, not of himself nor of his fellow Christians.

This last "correction" should not minimize the proud, joyful faith conviction which must distinguish Christians. They are redeemed people. God has set them free from sin, futility and "bondage to decay"; they are, already now, glorified children of God and predestined to participate in the eschatological glory of Christ. The Spirit of God, both first fruits and guarantee, dwells in them. The hostile world cannot endanger Christians from the outside. Being permitted and able to live out of such a conviction is for Christians a source of enduring joy.

Relevance for Christians Today

Because of the opposition between Spirit and "flesh" which we, modern Christians, too, are experiencing over and over again, we can understand, in some Pauline measure, what the weakness and conflict of the unredeemed person must be. Even if sufficient attention is given to the critical observations above, we recognize the fundamental correctness of Paul's discourse in Romans 7 in regard to the mystery of evil. Yet, more than in Paul's days, thanks to modern science, we must also relate that very personal inner division and conflict situation with more or less fixed, innate tendencies which the individual has inherited from past generations, as well as with the conditioning by both the non-transparent subconscious regions in the human person and the so determining influences from the social and cultural environment.

For our ecological sensitivity it has been positively surprising to see how Paul, in Romans 8, in his own specific manner deals with the (forlorn but hoped for) unity of creation. We came to the conclusion that Paul rightly focuses on the call and responsibility of the human person both in Romans 7 and 8. This should not be lost sight of in the midst of our just attention to present-day ethnological, sociological and psychological preoccupations.

The presence of God, Son and Spirit in Romans 7 and 8 make of these chapters a very rich passage of Scripture. This is also true because Paul speaks so penetratingly of the conflict situation of the unregenerate person and, thereafter, so enthusiastically of the liberation of Christians.

Nor must one forget to mention the time dimensions. In

Romans 7 Paul works out the miserable condition of the *past* and briefly announces the redemption which for the Christian has already occurred. In Romans 8 Paul deals with the life of the Christians in the *present*: they should not give in to the "flesh." By walking according to the Spirit they will please God and fulfill the just requirement of the law. Christians, however, will also share in the suffering of Christ; in their lifetime they will experience all kinds of hardships, but no adversity will be able to separate them from the love of God in Christ Jesus. Finally, Paul also speaks of the ultimate *future*: the perspective of life after death, the future resurrection of the body, the eschatological glorification which awaits Christians and will definitively conform them to the image of God's Son. Thanks to Christ, Christians are children of God and, with Christ, joint heirs of God. The Spirit of Christ urges them to call God "Abba! Father."

In our sixth chapter much attention was given to the structure of Romans 8:31-39. The structural analysis reveals to us the outstanding literary ability of its author. One hopes, however, that such a detailed analysis does not endanger our appreciation of the content quality of this text as a whole. For the conclusion of Romans 8 is the Christians' jubilant confidence of salvation which should lead them to faithfulness in everyday Christian life.

APPENDIX

FOUR MODERN TRANSLATIONS

As said in the Foreword, the biblical text used in this book is for the most part that of the New Revised Standard Version (NRSV). In this Appendix we present, together with this version, three other recent translations, the Revised English Bible (REB), the New American Bible (NAB) and the New International Version (NIV), verse after verse. The reader can easily compare them.

It must strike us that the REB is the freest translation (sometimes almost a paraphrase), that the NAB is not so different from the NRSV and that, as far as freedom is concerned, the NIV is somewhat in between the NRSV and the REB.

Some translations squarely avoid exclusive language: see, for example, 8:12: "brothers and sisters" (NRSV), "my friends" (REB); or compare the translations of 8:15 and 23.

The NRSV and NAB retain the term "flesh;" this is rendered in the REB and NIV by means of different expressions, such as "very nature," "sinful nature," "old nature," "unspiritual nature," "(my) unspiritual self," "sinful mind." The adjective "fleshly" of 7:14b is translated by "of the flesh" (NRSV), "unspiritual" (REB and NIV), and "carnal" (NAB).

A comparison with regard to the different use of the capital for *pneuma* in chapter eight may prove to be interesting.

We may mention a few more data.
– In 7:9, the NRSV has "sin revived," the REB and NIV have "sin sprang to life" and NAB writes "sin became alive."
– Both the REB and NAB translate *nomos* in 7:21 by "principle" (the NAB employs the same term also in 7:23).
– In 7:25 the expression *autos egô* is rendered by the simple "I" (NRSV), by "left to myself" (REB) and by "I myself" (NAB and NIV).
– Attention must be given to the translation of "a sin offering" in

8:3 (only NIV, but also mentioned as a possiblity in footnote by NRSV and REB).
– In 8:20 *mataiotês* is "futility" for the NRSV and NAB, "frustration" for the REB and NIV; in 8:21 the expression *hê phthora tês douleias* becomes "the bondage to decay" in the NRSV and NIV, "the shackles of mortality" in the REB (see "mortality" also in v. 23, REB) and "the slavery to corruption" in the NAB.
– We should compare the end of 8:26: the Spirit himself intercedes "with sighs too deep for words" (NRSV), "through our (!) inarticulate groans" (REB), "with inexpressible groanings" (NAB), "with groans that words cannot express" (NIV).
– Finally, it is noteworthy that all four translations prefer statements in 8:33b and 8:34b for their main text, not questions as we do.

Here follow the four translations:

Romans 7:7-12

7   NRSV   What then should we say? That the law is sin? By no means! Yet, if it had not been for the law, I would not have known sin. I would not have known what it is to covet if the law had not said, "You shall not covet."

REB   What follows? Is the law identical with sin? Of course not! Yet had it not been for the law I should not have become acquainted with sin. For example, I should never have known what it was to covet, if the law had not said, "You shall not covet."

NAB   What then can we say? That the law is sin? Of course not! Yet I did not know sin except through the law, and I did not know what it is to covet except that the law said, "You shall not covet."

NIV   What shall we say, then? Is the law sin? Certainly not! Indeed I would not have known what sin was except through the law. For I would not have known what it was to covet if the law had not said, "Do not covet."

8   NRSV   But sin, seizing an opportunity in the commandment, produced in me all kinds of covetousness. Apart from the law sin lies dead.

REB   Through that commandment sin found its opportunity, and produced in me all kinds of wrong desires. In the absence of law, sin is devoid of life.

NAB But sin, finding an opportunity in the commandment, produced in me every kind of covetousness. Apart from the law sin is dead.

NIV But sin, seizing the opportunity afforded by the commandment, produced in me every kind of covetous desire. For apart from law, sin is dead.

9 NRSV I was once alive apart from the law, but when the commandment came, sin revived

REB There was a time when, in the absence of law, I was fully alive; but when the commandment came, sin sprang to life and I died.

NAB I once lived outside the law, but when the commandment came, sin became alive;

NIV Once I was alive apart from law; but when the commandment came, sin sprang to life and I died.

10 NRSV and I died, and the very commandment that promised life proved to be death to me.

REB The commandment which should have led to life proved in my experience to lead to death,

NAB then I died, and the commandment that was for life turned out to be death for me.

NIV I found that the very commandment that was intended to bring life actually brought death.

11 NRSV For sin, seizing an opportunity in the commandment, deceived me and through it killed me.

REB because in the commandment sin found its opportunity to seduce me, and through the commandment killed me.

NAB For sin, seizing an opportunity in the commandment, deceived me and through it put me to death.

NIV For sin, seizing the opportunity afforded by the commandment, deceived me, and through the commandment put me to death.

12 NRSV So the law is holy, and the commandment is holy and just and good.

REB So then, the law in itself is holy and the commandment is holy and just and good.

NAB So then the law is holy, and the commandment is holy and righteous and good.

NIV So then, the law is holy, and the commandment is holy, righteous and good.

Romans 7:13-25

13 NRSV Did what is good, then, bring death to me? By no means! It was sin, working death in me through what is good, in order that sin might be shown to be sin, and through the commandment might become sinful beyond measure.

REB Are we therefore to say that this good thing caused my death? Of course not! It was sin that killed me, and thereby sin exposed its true character: it used a good thing to bring about my death, and so, through the commandment, sin became more sinful than ever.

NAB Did the good, then, become death for me? Of course not! Sin, in order that it might be shown to be sin, worked death in me through the good, so that sin might become sinful beyond measure through the commandment.

NIV Did that which is good, then, become death to me? By no means! But in order that sin might be recognised as sin, it produced death in me through what was good, so that through the commandment sin might become utterly sinful.

14 NRSV For we know that the law is spiritual; but I am of the flesh, sold into slavery under sin.

REB We know that the law is spiritual; but I am not: I am unspiritual, sold as a slave to sin.

NAB We know that the law is spiritual; but I am carnal, sold into slavery to sin.

NIV We know that the law is spiritual; but I am unspiritual, sold as a slave to sin.

15 NRSV I do not understand my own actions. For I do not do what I want, but I do the very thing I hate.

REB I do not even acknowledge my own actions as mine, for what I do is not what I want to do, but what I detest.

NAB What I do, I do not understand. For I do not do what I want, but I do what I hate.

NIV I do not understand what I do. For what I want to do I do not do, but what I hate I do.

16 NRSV Now if I do what I do not want, I agree that the law is good.

REB But if what I do is against my will, then clearly I agree with the law and hold it to be admirable.

NAB Now if I do what I do not want, I concur that the law is good.

NIV And if I do what I do not want to do, I agree that the law is good.

17 NRSV But in fact it is no longer I that do it, but sin that dwells within me.

REB This means that it is no longer I who perform the action, but sin that dwells in me.

NAB So now it is no longer I who do it, but sin that dwells in me.

NIV As it is, it is no longer I myself who do it, but it is sin living in me.

18 NRSV For I know that nothing good dwells within me, that is, in my flesh. I can will what is right, but I cannot do it.

REB For I know that nothing good dwells in me — my unspiritual self, I mean — for though the will to do good is there, the ability to effect it is not.

NAB For I know that good does not dwell in me, that is, in my flesh. The willing is ready at hand, but doing the good is not.

NIV I know that nothing good lives in me, that is, in my sinful nature. For I have the desire to do what is good, but I cannot carry it out.

19 NRSV For I do not do the good I want, but the evil I do not want is what I do.

REB The good which I want to do, I fail to do; but what I do is the wrong which is against my will;

NAB For I do not do the good I want, but I do the evil I do not want.

NIV For what I do is not the good I want to do; no, the evil I do not want to do — this I keep on doing.

20 NRSV   Now if I do what I do not want, it is no longer I that do it, but sin that dwells within me.
   REB   and if what I do is against my will, clearly it is no longer I who am the agent, but sin that has its dwelling in me.
   NAB   Now if I do what I do not want, it is no longer I who do it, but sin that dwells in me.
   NIV   Now if I do what I do not want to do, it is no longer I who do it, but it is sin living in me that does it.

21 NRSV   So I find it to be a law that when I want to do what is good, evil lies close at hand.
   REB   I discover this principle, then: that when I want to do right, only wrong is within my reach.
   NAB   So, then, I discover the principle that when I want to do right, evil is at hand.
   NIV   So I find this law at work: When I want to do good, evil is right there with me.

22 NRSV   For I delight in the law of God in my inmost self,
   REB   In my inmost self I delight in the law of God,
   NAB   For I take delight in the law of God, in my inner self.
   NIV   For in my inner being I delight in God's law;

23 NRSV   but I see in my members another law at war with the law of my mind, making me captive to the law of sin that dwells in my members.
   REB   but I perceive in my outward actions a different law, fighting against the law that my mind approves, and making me a prisoner under the law of sin which controls my conduct.
   NAB   but I see in my members another principle at war with the law of my mind, taking me captive to the law of sin that dwells in my members.
   NIV   but I see another law at work in the members of my body, waging war against the law of my mind and making me a prisoner of the law of sin at work within my members.

24 NRSV   Wretched man that I am! Who will rescue me from this body of death?
   REB   Wretched creature that I am, who is there to rescue me from this state of death?

NAB Miserable one that I am! Who will deliver me from this mortal body?

NIV What a wretched man I am! Who will rescue me from this body of death?

25 **NRSV** Thanks be to God through Jesus Christ our Lord! So then, with my mind I am a slave to the law of God, but with my flesh I am a slave to the law of sin.

REB Who but God? Thanks be to him through Jesus Christ our Lord! To sum up then: left to myself I serve God's law with my mind, but with my unspiritual nature I serve the law of sin.

NAB Thanks be to God through Jesus Christ our Lord. Therefore, I myself, with my mind, serve the law of God but, with my flesh, the law of sin.

NIV Thanks be to God — through Jesus Christ our Lord! So then, I myself in my mind am a slave to God's law, but in the sinful nature a slave to the law of sin.

Romans 8:1-17

1 **NRSV** There is therefore now no condemnation for those who are in Christ Jesus.

REB It follows that there is now no condemnation for those who are united with Christ Jesus.

NAB Hence, now there is no condemnation for those who are in Christ Jesus.

NIV Therefore, there is now no condemnation for those who are in Christ Jesus,

2 **NRSV** For the law of the Spirit of life in Christ Jesus has set you free from the law of sin and of death.

REB In Christ Jesus the life-giving law of the Spirit has set you free from the law of sin and death.

NAB For the law of the spirit of life in Christ Jesus has freed you from the law of sin and death.

NIV because through Christ Jesus the law of the Spirit of life set me free from the law of sin and death.

3 **NRSV** For God has done what the law, weakened by the

flesh, could not do: by sending his own Son in the likeness of sinful flesh, and to deal with sin, he condemned sin in the flesh,

REB What the law could not do, because of human weakness robbed it of all potency, God has done: by sending his own Son in the likeness of our sinful nature and to deal with sin, he has passed judgement against sin within that very nature,

NAB For what the law, weakened by the flesh, was powerless to do, this God has done: by sending his own Son in the likeness of sinful flesh and for the sake of sin, he condemned sin in the flesh,

NIV For what the law was powerless to do in that it was weakened by the sinful nature, God did by sending his own Son in the likeness of sinful man to be a sin offering. And so he condemned sin in sinful man,

4 NRSV so that the just requirement of the law might be fulfilled in us, who walk not according to the flesh but according to the Spirit.

REB so that the commandment of the law may find fulfilment in us, whose conduct is no longer controlled by the old nature, but by the Spirit.

NAB so that the righteous decree of the law might be fulfilled in us, who live not according to the flesh but according to the spirit.

NIV in order that the righteous requirements of the law might be fully met in us, who do not live according to the sinful nature but according to the Spirit.

5 NRSV For those who live according to the flesh set their minds on the things of the flesh, but those who live according to the Spirit set their minds on the things of the Spirit.

REB Those who live on the level of the old nature have their outlook formed by it, and that spells death; but those who live on the level of the spirit have the spiritual outlook, and that is life and peace.

NAB For those who live according to the flesh are concerned with the things of the flesh, but those who live according to the spirit with the things of the spirit.

NIV Those who live according to the sinful nature have their minds set on what that nature desires; but those who live in accordance with the Spirit have their minds set on what the Spirit desires.

6 NRSV To set the mind on the flesh is death, but to set the mind on the Spirit is life and peace.

REB (see verse 5)

NAB The concern of the flesh is death, but the concern of the spirit is life and peace.

NIV The mind of sinful man is death, but the mind controlled by the Spirit is life and peace,

7 NRSV For this reason the mind that is set on the flesh is hostile to God; it does not submit to God's law — indeed it cannot,

REB For the outlook of the unspiritual nature is enmity with God; it is not subject to the law of God and indeed it cannot be;

NAB For the concern of the flesh is hostility toward God; it does not submit to the law of God, nor can it;

NIV because the sinful mind is hostile to God. It does not submit to God's law, nor can it do so.

8 NRSV and those who are in the flesh cannot please God.

REB those who live under its control cannot please God.

NAB and those who are in the flesh cannot please God.

NIV Those controlled by the sinful nature cannot please God.

9 NRSV But you are not in the flesh; you are in the Spirit, since the Spirit of God dwells in you. Anyone who does not have the Spirit of Christ does not belong to him.

REB But you do not live like that. You live by the spirit, since God's Spirit dwells in you; and anyone who does not possess the Spirit of Christ does not belong to Christ.

NAB But you are not in the flesh; on the contrary, you are in the spirit, if only the Spirit of God dwells in you. Whoever does no have the Spirit of Christ does not belong to him.

NIV You, however, are controlled not by the sinful nature but by the Spirit, if the Spirit of God lives in you. And if anyone does not have the Spirit of Christ, he does not belong to Christ.

10   NRSV   But if Christ is in you, though the body is dead because of sin, the Spirit is life because of righteousness.
REB   But if Christ is in you, then although the body is dead because of sin, yet the Spirit is your life because you have been justified.
NAB   But if Christ is in you, although the body is dead because of sin, the spirit is alive because of righteousness.
NIV   But if Christ is in you, your body is dead because of sin, yet your spirit is alive because of righteousness.

11   NRSV   If the Spirit of him who raised Jesus from the dead dwells in you, he who raised Christ from the dead will give life to your mortal bodies also through his Spirit that dwells in you.
REB   Moreover, if the Spirit of him who raised Jesus from the dead dwells in you, then the God who raised Christ Jesus from the dead will also give new life to your mortal bodies through his indwelling Spirit.
NAB   If the Spirit of the one who raised Jesus from the dead dwells in you, the one who raised Christ from the dead will give life to your mortal bodies also, through his Spirit that dwells in you.
NIV   And if the Spirit of him who raised Jesus from the dead is living in you, he who raised Christ from the dead will also give life to your mortal bodies through his Spirit, who lives in you.

12   NRSV   So then, brothers and sisters, we are debtors, not to the flesh, to live according to the flesh —
REB   It follows, my friends, that our old nature has no claim on us; we are not obliged to live in that way.
NAB   Consequently, brothers, we are not debtors to the flesh, to live according to the flesh.
NIV   Therefore, brothers, we have an obligation — but it is not to the sinful nature, to live according to it.

13   NRSV   for if you live according to the flesh, you will die; but if by the Spirit you put to death the deeds of the body, you will live.
REB   If you do so, you must die. But if by the Spirit you put to death the base pursuits of the body, then you will live.

NAB For if you live according to the flesh, you will die, but if by the spirit you put to death the deeds of the body, you will live.

NIV For if you live according to the sinful nature, you will die; but if by the Spirit you put to death the misdeeds of the body, you will live,

14 **NRSV** For all who are led by the Spirit of God are children of God.

REB For all who are led by the Spirit of God are sons of God.

NAB For those who are led by the Spirit of God are children of God.

NIV because those who are led by the Spirit of God are sons of God.

15 **NRSV** For you did not receive a spirit of slavery to fall back into fear, but you have received a spirit of adoption. When we cry, "Abba! Father!"

REB The Spirit you have received is not a spirit of slavery, leading you back into a life of fear, but a Spirit of adoption, enabling us to cry "Abba! Father!"

NAB For you did not receive a spirit of slavery to fall back into fear, but you received a spirit of adoption, through which we cry, "Abba, Father!"

NIV For you did not receive a spirit that makes you a slave again to fear, but you received the Spirit of sonship. And by him we cry, "Abba, Father."

16 **NRSV** it is that very Spirit bearing witness with our spirit that we are children of God,

REB The Spirit of God affirms to our spirit that we are God's children;

NAB The Spirit itself bears witness with our spirit that we are children of God,

NIV The Spirit himself testifies with our spirit that we are God's children.

17 **NRSV** and if children, then heirs, heirs of God and joint heirs with Christ — if, in fact, we suffer with him so that we may also be glorified with him.

REB and if children, then heirs, heirs of God and fellow-heirs with Christ; but we must share his sufferings if we are also to share his glory.

NAB and if children, then heirs, heirs of God and joint heirs with Christ, if only we suffer with him so that we may also be glorified with him.

NIV Now if we are children, then we are heirs — heirs of God and co-heirs with Christ, if indeed we share in his sufferings in order that we may also share in his glory.

Romans 8:18-30

18 NRSV I consider that the sufferings of this present time are not worth comparing with the glory about to be revealed to us.

REB For I reckon that the sufferings we now endure bear no comparison with the glory, as yet unrevealed, which is in store for us.

NAB I consider that the sufferings of this present time are as nothing compared with the glory to be revealed for us.

NIV I consider that our present sufferings are not worth comparing with the glory that will be revealed in us.

19 NRSV For the creation waits with eager longing for the revealing of the children of God;

REB The created universe is waiting with eager expectation for God's sons to be revealed.

NAB For creation awaits with eager expectation the revelation of the children of God;

NIV The creation waits in eager expectation for the sons of God to be revealed.

20 NRSV for the creation was subjected to futility, not of its own will but by the will of the one who subjected it, in hope

REB It was made subject to frustration, not of its own choice but by the will of him who subjected it, yet with the hope

NAB for creation was made subject to futility, not of its own accord but because of the one who subjected it, in hope

NIV For the creation was subjected to frustration, not by its own choice, but by the will of the one who subjected it, in hope

21 NRSV that the creation itself will be set free from its bondage to decay and will obtain the freedom of the glory of the children of God.

REB that the universe itself is to be freed from the shackles of mortality and is to enter upon the glorious liberty of the children of God.

NAB that creation itself would be set free from slavery to corruption and share in the glorious freedom of the children of God.

NIV that the creation itself will be liberated from its bondage to decay and brought into the glorious freedom of the children of God.

22 NRSV We know that the whole creation has been groaning in labor pains until now;

REB Up to the present, as we know, the whole created universe in all its parts groans as if in the pangs of childbirth.

NAB We know that all creation is groaning in labor pains even until now;

NIV We know that the whole creation has been groaning as in the pains of childbirth right up to the present time.

23 NRSV and not only the whole creation, but we ourselves, who have the first fruits of the Spirit, groan inwardly while we wait for adoption, the redemption of our bodies.

REB What is more, we also, to whom the Spirit is given as the firstfruits of the harvest to come, are groaning inwardly while we look forward eagerly to our adoption, our liberation from mortality.

NAB and not only that, but we ourselves, who have the firstfruits of the Spirit, we also groan within ourselves as we wait for adoption, the redemption of our bodies.

NIV Not only so, but we ourselves, who have the firstfruits of the Spirit, groan inwardly as we wait eagerly for our adoption as sons, the redemption of our bodies.

24 NRSV For in hope we were saved. Now hope that is seen is not hope. For who hopes for what is seen?

REB It was with this hope that we were saved. Now to see something is no longer to hope: why hope for what is already seen?

NAB For in hope we were saved. Now hope that sees for itself is not hope. For who hopes for what one sees?

NIV For in this hope we were saved. But hope that is seen is no hope at all. Who hopes for what he already has?

25 NRSV But if we hope for what we do not see, we wait for it with patience.

REB But if we hope for something we do not yet see, then we look forward to it eagerly and with patience.

NAB But if we hope for what we do not see, we wait with endurance.

NIV But if we hope for what we do not yet have, we wait for it patiently.

26 NRSV Likewise the Spirit helps us in our weakness; for we do not know how to pray as we ought, but that very Spirit intercedes with sighs too deep for words.

REB In the same way the Spirit comes to the aid of our weakness. We do not even know how we ought to pray, but through our inarticulate groans the Spirit himself is pleading for us,

NAB In the same way, the Spirit too comes to the aid of our weakness; for we do not know how to pray as we ought, but the Spirit itself intercedes with inexpressible groanings.

NIV In the same way, the Spirit helps us in our weakness. We do not know what we ought to pray, but the Spirit himself intercedes for us with groans that words cannot express.

27 NRSV And God, who searches the heart, knows what is the mind of the Spirit, because the Spirit intercedes for the saints according to the will of God.

REB and God who searches our inmost being knows what the Spirit means, because he pleads for God's people as God himself wills;

NAB And the one who searches hearts knows what is the intention of the Spirit, because it intercedes for the holy ones according to God's will.

NIV And he who searches our hearts knows the mind of the Spirit, because the Spirit intercedes for the saints in accordance with God's will.

28 NRSV We know that all things work together for good for those who love God, who are called according to his purpose.
  REB and in everything, as we know, he co-operates for good with those who love God and are called according to his purpose.
  NAB We know that all things work for good for those who love God, who are called according to his purpose.
  NIV And we know that in all things God works for the good of those who love him, who have been called according to his purpose.

29 NRSV For those whom he foreknew he also predestined to be conformed to the image of his Son, in order that he might be the firstborn within a large family.
  REB For those whom God knew before ever they were, he also ordained to share the likeness of his Son, so that he might be the eldest among a large family of brothers;
  NAB For those he foreknew he also predestined to be conformed to the image of his Son, so that the might be the firstborn among many brothers.
  NIV For those God foreknew he also predestined to be conformed to the likeness of his Son, that he might be the firstborn among many brothers.

30 NRSV And those whom he predestined he also called; and those whom he called he also justified; and those whom he justified he also glorified.
  REB and those whom he foreordained, he also called, and those whom he called he also justified, and those whom he justified he also glorified.
  NAB And those he predestined he also called; and those he called he also justified; and those he justified he also glorified.
  NIV And those he predestined, he also called; those he called, he also justified; those he justified, he also glorified.

Romans 8:31-39

31 NRSV What then are we to say about these things? If God is for us, who is against us?
  REB With all this in mind, what are we to say? If God is on our side, who is against us?

NAB   What then shall we say to this? If God is for us, who can be against us?

NIV   What, then, shall we say in response to this? If God is for us, who can be against us?

32   NRSV   He who did withhold his own Son, but gave him up for all of us, will he not with him also give us everything else?

REB   He did not spare his own Son, but gave him up for us all; how can he fail to lavish every other gift upon us?

NAB   He who did not spare his own Son but handed him over for us all, how will he not also give us everything else along with him?

NIV   He who did not spare his own Son, but gave him up for us all — how will he not also, along with him, graciously give us all things?

33   NRSV   Who will bring any charge against God's elect? It is God who justifies.

REB   Who will bring a charge against those whom God has chosen? Not God, who acquits!

NAB   Who will bring a charge against God's chosen ones? It is God who acquits us.

NIV   Who will bring any charge against those whom God has chosen? It is God who justifies.

34   NRSV   Who is to condemn? It is Christ Jesus, who died, yes, who was raised, who is at the right hand of God, who indeed intercedes for us.

REB   Who will pronounce judgement? Not Christ, who died, or rather rose again; not Christ, who is at God's right hand and pleads our cause!

NAB   Who will condemn? It is Christ [Jesus] who died, rather, was raised, who also is at the right hand of God, who indeed intercedes for us.

NIV   Who is he that condemns? Christ Jesus, who died — more than that, who was raised to life — is at the right hand of God and is also interceding for us.

35   NRSV   Who will separate us from the love of Christ? Will hardship, or distress, or persecution, or famine, or nakedness, or peril, or sword?

REB   Then what can separate us from the love of Christ? Can affliction or hardship? Can persecution, hunger, nakedness, danger, or sword?

NAB   What will separate us from the love of God? Will anguish, or distress, or persecution, or famine, or nakedness, or peril, or the sword?

NIV   Who shall separate us from the love of Christ? Shall trouble or hardship or persecution or famine or nakedness or danger or sword?

36   NRSV   As it is written, "For your sake we are being killed all day long; we are accounted as sheep to be slaughtered."

REB   "We are being done to death for your sake all day long," as scripture says; "we have been treated like sheep for slaughter" -

NAB   As it is written: "For your sake we are being slain all the day; we are looked upon as sheep to be slaughtered."

NIV   As it is written: "For your sake we face death all day long; we are considered as sheep to be slaughtered."

37   NRSV   No, in all these things we are more than conquerors through him who loved us.

REB   and yet, throughout it all, overwhelming victory is ours through him who loved us.

NAB   No, in all these things we conquer overwhelmingly through him who loved us.

NIV   No, in all these things we are more than conquerors through him who loved us.

38   NRSV   For I am convinced that neither death, nor life, nor angels, nor rulers, nor things present, nor things to come, nor powers,

REB   For I am convinced that there is nothing in death or life, in the realm of spirits or superhuman powers, in the world as it is or the world as it shall be, in the forces of the universe,

NAB   For I am convinced that neither death, nor life, nor angels, nor principalities, nor present things, nor future things, nor powers,

NIV   For I am convinced that neither death nor life, neither angels nor demons, neither the present nor the future, nor any powers,

39 NRSV   nor height, nor depth, nor anything else will be able to separate us from the love of God in Christ Jesus our Lord.

REB   in heights or depths — nothing in all creation that can separate us from the love of God in Christ Jesus our Lord.

NAB   nor height, nor depth, nor any other creature will be able to separate us from the love of God in Christ Jesus our Lord.

NIV   neither height nor depth, nor anything else in all creation, will be able to separate us from the love of God that is in Christ Jesus our Lord.

BIBLIOGRAPHY

Achtemeier, Paul, J., "'Some Things in Them Hard to Understand.' Reflections on an Approach to Paul," *Interpretation* 38 (1984) 254-267.

Baarlink, Heinrich, *Romeinen I. Een praktische bijbelverklaring* (Tekst en toelichting). Kampen: Kok, 1987.

Balz, Horst Robert, *Heilsvertrauen und Welterfahrung. Strukturen der paulinischen Eschatologie nach Römer 8,18-39* (Beiträge zur evangelischen Theologie, 59). Munich: Kaiser, 1971.

Barrett, Charles Kingsley, *A Commentary on the Epistle to the Romans* (BNTC/HNTC). London: Black - New York: Harper, 1957.

Benoit, Pierre, "La Loi et la Croix d'après Saint Paul (Rom. VII,7 - VIII,4)," *Revue biblique* 47 (1938) 481-509.

Benoit, Pierre, "Nous gémissons attendant la délivrance de notre corps (Rom. 8,23)," *Recherches de science religieuse* 39 (1951-52) 267-280.

Bergmeier, Roland, "Röm 7,7-25a (8,2): Der Mensch - das Gesetz - Gott - Paulus - die Exegese im Widerspruch?" *Kerygma und Dogma* 31 (1985) 162-172.

Bindemann, Walther, *Die Hoffnung der Schöpfung. Römer 8,18-27 und die Frage einer Theologie der Befreiung von Mensch und Natur* (Neukirchener Studienbücher, 14). Neukirchen-Vluyn: Neukirchener Verlag, 1983.

Blank, Josef, "Gesetz und Geist," in L. De Lorenzi, ed., *The Law of the Spirit*, pp. 73-100 (discussion on pp. 100-127).

Blank, Josef, "Der gespaltene Mensch. Zur Exegese von Röm 7,7-25," *Bibel und Leben* 9 (1968) 10-20, also in Blank, *Schriftauslegung in Theorie und Praxis* (Bibl. Handbibliothek, 5). Munich: Kösel, 1969, pp. 158-173; also in Blank, *Paulus: Von Jesus zum Urchristentum*. Munich: Kösel, 1982, pp. 87-104.

Bornkamm, Günther, "Sin, Law and Death (Romans 7)," in

Bornkamm, *Early Christian Experience*. London: SCM, 1969, pp. 87-104.
Bouwman, Gijs, *Paulus aan de Romeinen. Een retorische analyse van Rom. 1-8* (Cahiers voor levensverdieping, 32). Averbode: Altiora, 1980.
Branick, Vincent P., "The Sinful Flesh of the Son of God (Rom 8:3): A Key Image of Pauline Theology," *Catholic Biblical Quarterly* 47 (1985) 246-262.
Bultmann, Rudolf, *Römer 7 und die Anthroplogie des Paulus*, in *Imago Dei. Beiträge zur theologischen Anthropologie. Festschrift G. Krüger*. Giessen: Töpelmann, 1932, pp. 53-62; also in Bultmann, *Exegetica*. Tübingen: Mohr, 1987, pp. 198-209.
Byrne, Brendan, "Living out the Righteousness of God: The Contribution of Rom 6:1-8:13 to an Understanding of Paul's Ethical Presuppositions," *Catholic Biblical Quarterly* 43 (1981) 557-581.

Cambier, Jules, "Le 'moi' dans Rom 7," in L. De Lorenzi, ed., *The Law of the Spirit*, pp. 13-44 (discussion on pp. 44-72).
Collins, Raymond E., *Christian Morality: Biblical Foundations*. Notre Dame, IN: Univ. Notre Dame Press, 1986, pp. 239-253: "And Why Not Do Evil That Good May Come."
Cranfield, C.E.B., *A Critical and Exegetical Commentary on the Epistle to the Romans*, 1 (ICC). Edinburgh: Clark, 1975.
Cranfield, C.E.B., "Some Observations on Romans 8:19-21," in R. Banks, ed., *Reconciliation and Hope. Festschrift L.L. Morris*. Grand Rapids, MI: Eerdmans, 1974, pp. 224-230.

De Kruijf, T.C., *De brief van Paulus aan de Romeinen* (Het Nieuwe Testament). Boxtel: Katholieke Bijbelstichting, 1986.
de la Potterie, Ignace, "Le chrétien conduit par l'Esprit dans son cheminement eschatologique (Rom 8,14)," in L. De Lorenzi, ed., *The Law of the Spirit*, pp. 209-241 (discussion on pp. 241-278).
De Lorenzi, Lorenzo, ed., *The Law of the Spirit in Rom 7 and 8* (Benedictina, 1). Rome: Saint Paul's Abbey, 1976.
Denton, D.R., "Apokaradokia," *Zeitschrift für die neutestamentliche Wissenschaft* 73 (1982) 138-140.
Dunn, James D.G., *Romans 1-8* (WBC). Dallas, TX: Word, 1988.

Dunn, James D.G., "Rom. 7,14-25 in the Theology of Paul," *Theologische Zeitschrift* 31 (1975) 257-273.

Espy, John M., "Paul's 'Robust Conscience' Re-examined," *New Testament Studies* 31 (1985) 161-188.

Fiedler, Peter, "Röm 8,31-39 als Brennpunkt paulinischer Frohbotschaft," *Zeitschrift fur die neutestestamentliche Wissenschaft* 68 (1977) 23-34.

Fung, Ronald Y.K., "The Impotence of the Law: Toward a Fresh Understanding of Romans 7:14-25," in W.W. Gasque and W.S. LaSor, eds., *Scripture, Tradition, and Interpretation. Festschrift E.F. Harrison*. Grand Rapids, MI: Eerdmans, 1978, pp. 34-48.

Grelot, Pierre, "La vie dans l'Esprit (d'après Romains 7-8)," *Christus* 29 (1982), nr. 113, pp. 83-98.

Grossouw, Willem K., "De verscheurde mens van Romeinen zeven," in *Vriendengave. Bernardus Kardinaal Alfrink aangeboden* .... Utrecht: Het Spectrum, 1964, pp. 68-80.

Guardini, Romano, *Drei Schriftlesungen*. Würzburg: Werkbund-Verlag, ²1958, pp. 69-94: "Das Harren der Schöpfung (Röm. 8,12-39)."

Gundry, Rorbert Horton, "The Moral Frustration of Paul before His Conversion: Sexual Lust in Romans 7:7-25," in D.A. Hagner and M.J. Harris, eds., *Pauline Studies. Festschrift F.F. Bruce*. Grand Rapids, MI: Eerdmans, 1980, pp. 228-245.

Houtman, Cornelis, *Wereld en tegenwereld*. Baarn: Kok, 1982.

Käsemann, Ernst, *An die Römer* (HNT). Göttingen: Vandenhoeck & Ruprecht, 1975.

Käsemann, Ernst, *Paulinische Perspektiven*. Tübingen: Mohr, 1969, pp. 211-236: "Der gottesdienstliche Schrei nach der Freiheit."

Kertelge, Karl, "Exegetische Überlegungen zum Verständnis der paulinischen Anthropologie nach Römer 7," *Zeitschrift für die neutestamentliche Wissenschaft* 62 (1971) 105-114.

Kümmel, Werner Georg, *Das Bild des Menschen im Neuen Testament* (AThANT, 13). Zurich: Zwingli, 1948; also in Kümmel, *Römer 7 und das Bild des Menschen im Neuen Testament. Zwei Studien* (Theologische Bücherei, 53). Munich: Kaiser, 1974, pp. 161-214.

Kümmel, Werner Georg, *Römer 7 und die Bekehrung des Paulus* (Untersuchungen zum Neuem Testament, 17). Leipzig: Hinrichs, 1929; also in Kümmel, *Römer 7 und das Bild* ..., pp. 1-160.

Kuss, Otto, *Der Römerbrief*, 2. Regensburg: Pustet, 1959.

Lagrange, Marie-Joseph., *Epître aux Romains*. Paris: Gabalda ³1922.

Lambrecht, Jan, "The Groaning Creation: A Study of Rom 8:18-30," *Louvain Studies* 15 (1990) 3-18.

Lambrecht, Jan, "Man Before and Without Christ: Rom 7 and Pauline Anthropology," *Louvain Studies* 5 (1974-75) 18-33.

Lambrecht, Jan and Richard W. Thompson, *Justification by Faith: The Implications of Romans 3:27-31* (Zacchaeus Studies: NT). Wilmington, DE: Glazier, 1989.

Langevin, Paul-Emile, "Exégèse et psychanalyse. Lecture psychanalytique de Romains VII et VIII," *Laval théologique et philosophique* 36 (1980) 129-137.

Lekkerkerker, Arie Frederik Nelis, *De brief van Paulus aan de Romeinen*, 1 (Prediking NT). Nijkerk: Callenbach, ²1971.

Lohse, Eduard, "Zur Analyse und Interpretation von Röm. 8,1-17," in L. De Lorenzi, ed., *The Law of the Spirit*, pp. 129-146 (discussion on pp. 147-166).

Lyonnet, Stanislas, "L'histoire du salut selon le chapitre VII de l'Epître aux Romains," *Biblica* 43 (1962) 117-151.

Lyonnet, Stanislas, "La rédemption de l'Univers," *Lumière et vie* 48 (1960) 43-62.

Lyonnet, Stanislas, "'Tu ne convoiteras pas' (Rom 7,7)," in *Neotestamentica et patristica. Festschrift O. Cullmann* (Suppl. Nov. Test., 6). Leiden: Brill, 1962, pp. 157-165.

Martin, Brice L., "Some Reflections on the Identity of the 'ego' in Rom 7:14-25," *Scottish Journal of Theology* 34 (1981) 39-47.

Michel, Otto, *Der Brief an die Römer* (KEK). Göttingen: Vandenhoeck & Ruprecht, ⁵1978.
Modalsli, Ole, "Gal. 2,19-21; 5,16-18 und Röm. 7,7-25," *Theologische Zeitschrift* 21 (1965) 22-37.
Moo, Douglas J., "Israel and Paul in Romans 7.7-12," *New Testament Studies* 32 (1986) 122-135.
Murray, John, *The Epistle to the Romans*, 1 (New Intern. Comm.), Grand Rapids, MI: Eerdmans, 1959.

Obeng, E.A., "The Reconciliation of Rom. 8,26f. to the New Testament Writings and Themes," *Scottish Journal of Theology* 39 (1986) 165-174.
Obeng, E.A., "The Origins of the Spirit Intercession Motif in Romans 8.26," *New Testament Studies* 32 (1986) 621-632.

Paulsen, Henning, *Überlieferung und Auslegung in Römer 8* (WMANT, 43). Neukirchen: Neukirchener Verlag, 1974.
Pesch, Rudolf, *Römerbrief* (Die neue Echter Bibel). Würzburg: Echter, 1983.

Räisänen, Heikki, "Zum Gebrauch von EPITHYMIA und EPITHYMEIN bei Paulus," *Studia theologica* 33 (1979) 85-99; also in Räisänen, *The Torah and Christ*. Helsinki: Finnish Exegetical Society, 1986, pp. 148-167.
Räisänen, Heikki, "Sprachliches zum Spiel des Paulus mit NOMOS," in Räisänen, *Torah*, pp. 119-147.
Ridderbos, Herman, *Aan de Romeinen* (Comm. NT). Kampen: Kok, 1959.
Ridderbos, H., *Paul: An Outline of His Theology*. London: SPCK, 1966, pp. 153-160.

Sanday, William and Arthur Cayley Headlam, *The Epistle to the Romans* (ICC). Edinburgh: Clark, ⁵1902.
Sanders, E.P., "Romans 7 and the Purpose of the Law," *Proceedings of the Irish Biblical Association* 7 (1983) 44-59.
Schlier, Heinrich, *Der Römerbrief* (HTKNT), Freiburg-Basel-Vienna: Herder, 1977.
Schlier, Heinrich, "Das, worauf alles wartet. Eine Auslegung von

Römer 8,18-30," in *Interpretation der Welt. Festschrift R. Guardini*. Würzburg: Echter, 1965, pp. 599-616.

Schnackenburg, Rudolf, "Römer 7 im Zusammenhang des Römerbriefes," in E.E. Ellis and E. Grässer, eds., *Jesus und Paulus. Festschrift W.G. Kümmel*. Göttingen: Vandenhoeck & Ruprecht, 1975, pp. 283-300.

Schottroff, Luise, "Die Schreckensherrschaft der Sünde und die Befreiung durch Christus nach der Römerbrief des Paulus," *Evangelische Theologie* 39 (1979) 497-510.

Segal, Alan F., "Romans and Jewish Dietary Law," *Studies in Religion/Sciences religieuses* 15 (1986) 361-674.

Sloan, Robert B., "Paul and the Law: Why the Law Cannot Save," *Novum Testamentum* 33 (1991) 35-60.

Theissen, Gerd, *Psychologische Aspekte paulinischer Theologie* (FRLANT, 131). Göttingen: Vandenhoeck & Ruprecht, 1983, especially pp. 181-268.

Van den Beld, A., "Romeinen 7:14-25 en het probeem van de Akrasía," *Bijdragen* 46 (1985) 39-57 (English summary on p. 58).

Van de Sandt, H.W.M., "An Explanation of Rom. 8,4a," in *Bijdragen* 37 (1976) 361-378.

Van de Sandt, H.W.M., "Research into Rom. 8,4a," *Bijdragen* 37 (1976) 252-269.

Vergote, Antoon, "Vie, loi et clivage du Moi dans l'épître aux Romains 7," in R. Barthes, P. Beauchamps ..., *Exégèse et herméneutique*. Paris: Seuil, 1971, pp. 109-147 (discussion on pp. 149-173).

Vögtle, Anton, "Röm. 8,19-22: eine schöpfungstheologische oder anthropologisch-soteriologische Aussage?" in A. Descamps and A. de Halleux, eds., *Mélanges bibliques en hommage au R.P. Rigaux*. Gembloux: Duculot, 1970, pp. 351-366; also in Vögtle, *Das Neue Testament und die Zukunft des Kosmos*. Düsseldorf: Patmos, 1973, pp. 183-208.

Vögtle, Anton, in L. De Lorenzi, ed., *The Law of the Spirit*, pp. 191-197 and 206-208.

von der Osten-Sacken, Peter, *Römer 8 als Beispiel paulinischer Soteriologie* (FRLANT, 122). Göttingen: Vandenhoeck & Ruprecht, 1975.

Wedderburn, A.J.W., "Romans 8.26 — Towards a Theology of Glossolalia?" *Scottish Journal of Theology* 28 (1975) 369-377.

Whiteley, Denys Edward Hugh, "Rom. 8,18-39: A Hermeneutical Approach," in L. De Lorenzi, ed., *The Law of the Spirit*, pp. 167-178 (discussion on pp. 178-208).

Wilckens, Ulrich, *Der Brief an die Römer*, 2 (EKK), Zurich: Benziger/Neukirchen-Vluyn: Neukirchener Verlag, 1980.

Zeller, Dieter, *Der Brief an die Römer* (Regensburger NT). Regensburg: Pustet, 1985.

Ziesler, John A., *Paul's Letter to the Romans* (TPI NT Comm.). London: SCM-Philadelphia: Trinity Press International, 1989.

Ziesler, John A., "The Role of the Tenth Commandment in Romans 7," *Journal for the Study of the New Testament* 33 (1988) 41-56.

ORIENTALISTE, P.B. 41, B-3000 Leuven